EXECUTIVE ETIQUETTE

EXECUTIVE ETIQUETTE

How to Make Your Way to the Top with Grace and Style

Marjabelle Young Stewart and Marian Faux

St. Martin's Press
New York

Library of Congress Cataloging-in-Publication Data

Stewart, Marjabelle Young.
   Executive etiquette.

   1. Business etiquette. 2. Executives. I. Faux,
Marian. II. Title.
HF5387.S73 1986   395'.52   85-25049
ISBN 0-312-27426-2 (pbk.)

To William E. Stewart, Esquire, Billy Stewart,
and E. Russell Anderson
              M.Y.S.

              For my parents
                 M.G.F.

Contents

Voice • Improving Diction • Reviewing Foreign
Words and Phrases • Reviewing Foreign Menu
Terms • Practicing—A Final Word

Planning the Lunch • Arriving at the Lunch •
Offering Special Amenities to Female Guests •
Organizing the Seating • Smoking and Not
Smoking • Ordering Drinks • Ordering Food •
Playing Host • Playing Guest • Introducing Bus-
iness During Lunch • Ending the Lunch • Enter-
taining on Premises • Entertaining at Private
Clubs • Entertaining on a Boat or Ship • Con-
ducting Other Business Entertainment • Host-
ing a Catered Function • Planning Purely Social
Entertaining

Planning the Party • Issuing Invitations • Host-
ing the Large Party • Hosting the Buffet Dinner
• Hosting the Informal Dinner • Hosting the
Formal Dinner • Hiring a Caterer for Home
Entertaining • Being the Host • Handling Chil-
dren at a Party • Determining the Price of Enter-
taining • Welcoming Unexpected Guests •
Choosing Appropriate Dress

Setting the Table • Handling Each Course •
Dining • Sitting Down • Excusing Yourself •
Using the Napkin • Making Conversation •
Talking to Persons Who Serve You • Reaching •

Asking for What You Need • Dealing with Pests in Food • Removing Food from Your Mouth • Eating Food That Is Too Hot • Using Catsup and Other Sauces • Using Jams, Jellies, and Butter • Stirring and Mashing Food • Using Bread to Clean the Plate • Drinking • Dealing with Dropped Silver or Food • Removing Dishes • Dealing with Food Spilled on the Table • Handling Used Flatware • Sharing Food • Smoking and Not Smoking • Eating Tricky Foods

Intimacies—Accepting and Rejecting Them •
Lunch with Colleagues • Client Relationships •
How to Get Credit for Work • Problems with
Other Women • Your Attitude • A Final Word

Expanding and Using Contacts • Using Execu-
tive Placement Services • Obtaining an Inter-
view • Dressing for the Interview • Knowing the
Etiquette of the Interview • Recognizing Inter-
view Tactics—Theirs and Yours • Playing
Down Humor • Acting Like a Team Player •
Showing Off Personal Strengths Graciously •
Talking About Problem Areas • Telling Little
Lies—When and How • Looking for That First
Job • Knowing Post-Interview Etiquette • Talk-
ing Salary and Benefits • Waiting to Start a New
Job • Using the Power to Hire and Fire Gra-
ciously

Giving Your Boss the News • Planning to Take
Your Leave • Giving and Attending Farewell
Celebrations • Maintaining Ties

Index

INTRODUCTION

B USINESS MANNERS today are in a state of flux as never before. One can no longer turn to the rules that worked twenty—or even ten—years ago. Formal and rigid in tone and outlook, they have little to do with the casual, liberated life styles that prevail today.

But one thing hasn't changed, and that is the fact that your actions and behavior will be observed (and duly noted) by those who have the power to promote you, and by those with the potential to hold you back—your secretaries, assistants, and fellow workers.

In everything you do in the office, whether it's writing a memo, giving an oral presentation, asking for a raise, or asking your assistant to type a letter, the manner in which you handle the situation portrays an image. If you're aiming for an executive-level position (or if you already have one and want to stay there), it's crucial that the image you portray is that of a poised, self-confident, successful executive. A large part of the success image comes from knowing the ins and outs of your particular business. But an even greater part comes from knowing the basics of good manners. Nothing builds confidence like knowing the rules of etiquette for every business situation—and knowing when it's proper and advantageous to break those rules. And nothing will build your success image faster than the ability to handle colleagues, clients, and superiors with tact and style.

There is little doubt that good manners can smooth the path to success. Good manners can lead to your promotion over an equally qualified but less poised rival. Good manners can lessen the awkwardness of such a rivalry, help you handle your superiors, help build better relationships with clients, and help establish your leadership potential. In fact, what you don't know about manners can hurt your chances of advancement, for no amount of technical skill can compensate for the inability to get along with others.

Several decades ago, John D. Rockefeller said, "The ability to get along with people is as purchasable a commodity as sugar and coffee, and I pay more for that ability than any under the sun." With the advent of the "me decade," however, top management began to lament the difficulty of finding outstanding people-handlers. One executive said, "Being able to work with others is the single most important characteristic a junior executive can have. I can always buy specialized knowledge, but it is sometimes a problem to find someone with good people sense, an ability to communicate well with others, to build their self-esteem." Another executive defined his personnel needs this way: "I don't care how intelligent my managers are; what I need most are people with people knowledge."

Good manners are essential in building good relationships with other people—and they can ensure that you have a steady supply of support and cooperation. Keeping the stress level high in an office may work for a while, but it rarely works in the long run. What does work over a long period of time is treating persons tactfully and graciously, recognizing their work, making them feel comfortable—in short, using good manners to make your way to the top. And that's what this book is all about.

Executive Etiquette was written for men and women on the rise in their professions, people who find themselves in business situations where they are expected to take the lead, whether in conducting a business meeting, entertaining an important client during a convention, or writing a well-planned business letter. It will show you how to get ahead using business manners, but most important, it presents manners realistically, showing what actually happens among most people in situations where good manners are called for and not what an ivory-tower expert thinks should happen. The art of afternoon tea will not be served up in this book, but good, solid business etiquette designed to promote careers will be.

All aspects of business manners are covered, from how to dress for various professions so the powers-that-be will know you are serious about advancement, to how to eat tricky foods and order an appropriate wine. It covers such subjects as how to speak and write correctly and intelligently, how to apply the etiquette of business travel and convention etiquette, how to manage business entertaining in the home and in restaurants—in short, all aspects of business where gracious manners can be put to work. Also included is a discussion of the emerging business (and social/sexual) etiquette among male and female professionals. There are special chapters on the etiquette of hiring and firing and the etiquette of landing a job. But most important, *Executive Etiquette* deals with the overall skill of getting along with others—of getting what you want from them—and getting to the top—through the use of tact and gracious manners.

M.Y.S.

CHAPTER 1

Daily Goodwill
in the Office

C AN THE ABILITY to get along with others be learned, or is it a trait that you are born with? While there are people who appear to be born charmers, most of us have to learn how to relate to others. And even the charmers often find that they have to refine their skills, particularly when they want to apply them to their professional life. Basically, though, getting along with others is largely a matter of courtesy, of sensing the needs of others and responding to them—of using the veneer of good manners that fuels polite society.

The ability to get along with others has its own rewards. Persons who work especially well with others quickly catch the eye of top management; they are ensured of the support of their colleagues and superiors, and if they play according to the rules of civility—which is what etiquette is all about—they are able to shine far more with their colleagues' support than they could without it.

The failure to promote goodwill in the office can hurt plenty. Bosses are persons who almost subconsciously take the pulse of relationships among their employees, and such readings do not always follow direct lines of authority. A boss may solicit his secretary's opinion of a junior executive; even if he does not do so directly, it may be offered, and he will probably listen.

If a colleague or even a subordinate is disgruntled with a co-worker, rest assured that he or she may well find a way to convey those views to top management. A wounded colleague may not even be out to get you but may only be responding to a threat to his or her sphere of authority. And in the long run, it simply is not in the best interests of management to promote someone who is disliked or who fails to command respect from coworkers. For this reason, goodwill among the people one works with can never be underestimated as a tool in upward mobility—and as a source of power.

Obviously, since business is basically a competitive operation, one will not always be able to keep a clear record with everyone. Fortunately, with good manners, you can handle even the awkward moments with grace.

DISCOVERING THE OFFICE CODE OF BEHAVIOR

The level of civility that exists in any office is fairly easy to detect in a short amount of time. Every office has a code of behavior that includes the manners that employees exhibit to one another. Of course, any etiquette book can list rules of etiquette toward coworkers, but a savvy employee needs to know how to balance this advice against the prevailing atmosphere. Too much formality in an office that does not call for it can make you look stuffy. And a lack of good manners toward fellow employees can make you dangerously unpopular.

In some offices, for example, first names are never used. In other offices, not to use first names is considered offensive. Like one stockbroker we know, you may be a person who cherishes your lunch hour as a private time, a time to collect yourself or to run errands. At one point in his career Jack Marshall discovered to his chagrin that he had taken a job with a brokerage firm where regular lunches with colleagues were expected. The lunches promoted camaraderie and were also an occasion for the informal conduct of business. Jack soon realized that his privacy break would have to take a back seat to the need to fraternize with his colleagues. Not to join them for lunch with some degree of regularity would make him appear standoffish and rude. Such was the unofficial code of good manners in this particular office.

EXTENDING GREETINGS

The manner in which persons who work in the same place greet each other varies from office to office. In a large advertising agency that occupies several floors of a highrise, coworkers may not even recognize each other on sight. In most companies, though, you do know most of your coworkers, and greeting them at least the first time you see them each day is a polite custom.

In some companies, particularly in the South, these greetings are often extended to an exchange of pleasantries; persons greet each other and may even stop to chat each time they meet.

You can and must decipher the pattern in your company and in your region of the country. You should make a point of greeting everyone known to you with at least a nod or a spoken word. Many subordinates wait for executives to take the lead in greeting them, so as an executive, you should be prepared to initiate greetings.

MAKING INTRODUCTIONS

The etiquette of making introductions has become less rigid in recent years, due to the more casual style that has pervaded all areas of American life, and due to the presence of more and more women in professional positions. Here are some general rules for making introductions:

When introducing two peers to each other, say: "Joan Porter, this is William Rathbone," or "Jack Jones, I would like you to meet Bill Bailey."

Generally a man is still presented to a woman; in business, this is definitely true if she holds a more prestigious position than he does. When a secretary or administrative assistant, male or female, is introduced to a superior, however, he or she is presented to the superior. This merely means you say the superior's name first, as follows: "Mr. Fox, I would like to introduce Joan Porter, my administrative assistant." In an informal office, the introduction might be: "Don Fox, I would like you to meet Joan Porter, my administrative assistant."

If you are introducing a new employee to fellow workers, it is nice to add a statement about the new person: "Dick Weber, I would like you to meet Sidney Smyth, who will be working with you in accounting."

Stuffy as it may sound, there is really only one appropriate way to acknowledge an introduction, and that is to say, very simply, "How do you do." Try not to say, "Pleased to meet you," "My pleasure," or "Pleased to make your acquaintance," all statements that may not be true ten minutes after you meet someone.

SHAKING HANDS

People shake hands more frequently today than they did years ago, and the rule about waiting for a woman to extend her hand has pretty much fallen by the wayside, with good reason. A man who is interviewing a woman as a potential employee or serving as host to her if she is a client would naturally be the one to extend his hand first today, and this is often exactly what occurs. On the other hand, a woman who wants to signal that she is to be treated the same way as her male contemporaries may show the initiative in shaking hands on occasions where she might not previously have extended her hand. What this means it that you should be prepared to shake hands with anyone you meet.

GREETING SOMEONE WHO ENTERS YOUR OFFICE

People stand when they are introduced to each other. There used to be a long list of rules about when to stand: men stood to meet each other and to meet women, women remained seated, and so forth. Today, the rules have shifted somewhat. Men still stand to meet each other; they still stand to meet a woman. And there is a growing tendency for women to stand when meeting another person these days. A woman who is greeting a client for a lunch she has planned may feel it is only appropriate to stand to greet that person, even if she is already seated at a table in a restaurant. On the other hand, many women retain the prerogative of remaining seated under these circumstances. Use whichever seems the more natural and gracious action toward the person whom you are greeting.

Younger persons have—and it is hoped, always will—deferred to older persons by standing to greet them, but, as with the custom of calling an older person Mr., Mrs., or Miss, this custom can have a cutting edge in one's professional life, and it is sometimes difficult to know when it is more tactful *not* to defer to a colleague on the basis of age. About the only honest answer is to play the situation by ear. If your company is very casual, or if a person with whom you deal has indicated anxiety about getting older or even seems vain about appearing young, it is probably more tactful not to stand. On the other hand, if yours is a company where the young executives show a great deal of deference to old hands, it is smarter to extend courtesies of this nature.

It is gracious to stand to greet anyone who comes into your office, with the exception of a secretary, assistant, or coworker who comes in regularly. Always stand to greet a visitor to the office. Colleagues frequently shake hands when they have not seen one another for a while, such as when someone returns from vacation or an extended business trip.

As soon as you have finished the greetings, motion the person to a nearby chair if the visitor is obviously going to stay.

DISMISSING OR ESCORTING SOMEONE LEAVING YOUR OFFICE

Usually the person to signal the end of a meeting is the one with greater power or prestige. A boss, for example, by gesture or word, dismisses an employee. Secretaries and clerical workers are especially accustomed to waiting for this gesture.

You can dismiss someone by simply nodding or thanking them for whatever information, material, or service they have just provided you with.

Dismissing a colleague requires more subtlety, and, of course, a colleague can also take leave whenever he or she wants to. Standing up often signals the end of the meeting between two colleagues.

Important visitors require red-carpet treatment. If you have time, it is gracious to walk someone out of your office to the elevator or stair. You can also simply walk him or her to the door of your office, or you can ask your secretary to show the person out. Never allow an important visitor to find the way out, especially if your office is in a maze of corridors.

There is, furthermore, an unspoken etiquette surrounding the order in which coworkers leave a room or go through a doorway. A young person always defers to a superior—in fact, observing a group of coworkers going through a door is a fairly good way to judge pecking order. Technically, a male boss can leave a room before a female secretary or administrative assistant, or even before a lower-ranking female executive, but in practice, these days men tend to defer to women on this issue.

SMOKING AND EATING IN AN OFFICE

The etiquette of smoking and eating is basically one of consideration for others. Do not smoke in someone's office without first asking his or her permission; the absence of an ash tray can frequently be taken as a sign that smoking is not appreciated.

In your own office, particularly if it is private, you may smoke as you like, but it is always considerate to ask any visitors if they mind your smoking before you light up.

It is never polite to eat in front of another person. If someone enters your office while you are indulging in a snack, the only civilized thing to do is to offer the visitor some; an equally civilized person will refuse your offer or take only a small portion. There is one obvious exception to this rule: if you are eating lunch at your desk when someone comes in, you need only stop eating until the person leaves. No one expects you to share a corned beef on rye with mustard.

ROLLING UP YOUR SLEEVES

There seems to be an unwritten code in each office about whether men shed their suit jackets, loosen their ties, and roll up their sleeves. You will have to decide for yourself whether any or all of these actions are appropriate, depending upon the atmosphere in the office where you work.

If you do any or all of these things, it is generally appropriate to unroll your shirt sleeves, put on your jacket, and tighten your tie when you leave the office, even if only to go to lunch. Again, the etiquette of what you put on or take off varies with the individual office.

NURTURING YOUR COLLEAGUES

When American life was simpler, colleagues had more in common and found it easier to be together. A group of young men hired right out of college to work as clerks in the billing department of a major accounting firm—in which they were sure to rise gradually to the top—found it relatively easy to relate to each other.

Relating to one's colleagues today is far more complex and fraught with opportunities for error. In part, this is because the competition is fiercer and the rewards are greater, but it is also because professional peers today tend to have widely disparate interests in and out of work, as well as a variety of levels of technical knowledge. Nevertheless, anyone who expects to climb the executive ladder cannot afford to ignore peer-group relationships. Maintaining good peer relationships is, in fact, an excellent way to be noticed by and earn the respect of top management.

There are three basic spheres in which you must learn to coexist with your peers—and there is an etiquette to each sphere. First, you must learn to be a gracious team player. Second, you must learn how to handle your rivals with tact. Third, it is important to show good manners and appreciation to those peers who are allies or friends.

Using Team Play

The arrangement of workers—usually junior executives and middle-management persons—into teams is a technique that has gained wide acceptance in well-managed companies. The underlying assumption of such organization is that the team players will subordinate their urges to compete for the sake of achieving collectively the task at hand. Teams are often used to implement long-term goals of a company or to solve especially difficult problems, so either the amount of time spent or the intensity of involvement with team players makes it necessary to cooperate, be gracious, and play the game with some degree of civility. Other books on business can provide information about the strategies of team play. In this book, we are primarily interested in the etiquette of team play, which, quite frankly, consists of how to promote yourself graciously while remaining a good team player.

Sometimes your interests will coincide with those of the other team members. Occasionally, they will not. In these instances, it is important to know how to look out for yourself while maintaining a veneer of good manners that will permit you to promote yourself even as you seem—and indeed, remain—a good team player. However important team play may appear in terms of the company's interests, never are you expected to submerge your self-interests for the sake of the team. You are only expected to depart graciously and according to a few rules of good manners.

Even on teams leaders emerge. There will be stars—and although all the team players may appear to function on an equal basis, it is a safe bet that the stars are more noticed—and more rewarded—than those who are strictly team players. It is also a safe bet that those stars make more money and are in line for bigger promotions than the nonstars.

The way to promote self-interest on a team is fairly simple: play fair with teammates, but take action to make sure you stand out from the group. Call attention to yourself, but do it politely by using your own fine manners, and none of your cohorts will be able to fault you, at least not publicly .

Without upsetting the aura of cooperation, you can use a basic strategy of self-promotion by producing memos playing up your role on the team, speaking up and speaking well at meetings, and asking for rewards for yourself when you have won individual recognition.

Consider the case of John Q., who was part of a four-person team designed to reorganize the sales division of a major corporation. Because the sales force was located in five regions throughout the country, someone would have to begin the study by doing a field survey on present conditions. This necessitated traveling with, talking with, and studying the sales force in action over a period of several months. Since all the persons on John's team had personal ties, and since all had responsibilities to other projects in the office, no one volunteered for this time-consuming task. Although the opportunity for glory was there, it seemed like a laborious way to achieve it. In addition, whoever volunteered for this task would be out of the office for two to three months—and that meant losing touch with the fast-paced political situation in the office. Three of the team members thought they could more readily advance themselves by staying in the office, letting someone else do what they viewed as tedious groundwork, and then moving in to play an integral role in the analytical process that would follow the information-gathering stage.

John Q., however, saw what he could do with such an assignment. For one thing, he had come up through the sales force, and he knew he could do an excellent job of information gathering based on his previous experiences. So he graciously volunteered for the task.

Before leaving to do the fieldwork, John Q. issued a long, detailed report to his boss, describing what he planned to do, how he planned to go about his task, what results he expected to bring in, and, incidentally, modestly pointed out why he was *the* most qualified person to do this job.

An added benefit that he had not anticipated was the closer relationship that resulted with his boss, who had also come up through the sales ranks and who consequently made the extra effort to talk more frequently by phone with John Q. than he did during an average week in the office. The boss even flew out to join John Q. one day in the field to show his support. His praises for John Q. were widely sung in the staff meeting the following week.

Knowing a good thing when he saw one, John Q. completed his assignment, waited ten days, and then went in to his boss to request a raise, *based on his additional effort on behalf of the team.* Of course, he got it.

John Q. did the correct thing by asking for a raise. Too often in team work, it is easy to think of oneself as belonging to the team and to think of rewards as coming to the entire team rather than to individuals. But all teams are made up of individuals. And, as we can see from the example of professional athletics, all the members of a team are not necessarily valued—or paid—equally.

The important aspect of team play is to cooperate only so long as you do not lose ground professionally, and then, when you must depart from the team's collective interests, to do so as graciously and politely as possible. This is an easy business maneuver to master since it is a rare teammate who will challenge you *if* you depart fairly. It isn't that someone won't want to challenge you; it is just that to do so will look mean-spirited, hostile, and rude.

While undertaking such a self-promotion effort, it is important to be especially courteous to team members. This is the time (in front of your boss) to make a point of how well a colleague handled a project, to back up a team member's idea in a meeting, to listen with extreme attention to whatever other team members are discussing. Extra efforts such as planning a dinner meeting with a cantankerous colleague or offering to work out a special problem over a couple of drinks after work will pay dividends in goodwill.

Finally, you must learn to depart from the team effort in order to set yourself apart as someone with leadership potential. The small signs of creativity are often what separate leaders from followers. For example, while you would never deliberately sabotage a meeting of the team, if you have an important and presumably brilliant suggestion about an action the team is recommending, don't bring it up in a team-planning session—bring it up during the big meeting with the boss. If you bring it up during the team meeting, everyone may jump on the bandwagon and you will have lost a valuable chance to show off your analytical skills. On the other hand, it is polite—to say nothing of cagey—to pretend when you introduce the idea that you only thought of it the night before.

Handling Rivals

Aggressive, competitive, and infighting rivals, the type referred to as "Type A" executives in one recent business book and as "jungle fighters" in another, do exist. And they can be treacherous. It may be some comfort to know that Type A executives rarely are found in the top ranks of management. A recent article* examined this issue and suggested three possible reasons for their absence at the top ranks: (1) their qualities of competitiveness and excessive drive may not be those needed at the upper echelon; (2) they may die off before reaching the top ranks; and (3) most important, they may threaten others so much that they are prevented, usually by their peers, from achieving their ultimate goals.

Still, these types exist, and it is a matter of survival to know how to handle a tough, overt competitor. Since you have already chosen to run a civilized race, it probably won't do any good to try to beat such a rival at his or her own game. You are probably not in top fighting form—not for the kind of fighting that jungle fighters engage in, anyway. There is, moreover, a way to handle treacherous rivals, and that is to beat them *at your own best game*—good manners and fair play. Almost any dirty tactic a rival uses, from starting rumors to antagonizing you in a meeting with a superior, can be countered with a round of polished manners.

In one Park Avenue law firm, where an associate was attempting to form compatible relations with her peers and with the partners who would judge the quality of her work, several problems arose.

The first problem involved a peer who also was Ms. Eaton's officemate. Mr. Addington was always at his desk when she arrived in the morning, and she felt that they held a nightly

* "Type A Manager," by J. Howard et al. *The Business Quarterly*, 42 :42−47 (Summer 1977).

contest to see who would work latest at the end of the day. Eaton, having worked several years before attending law school, compared her experience in the world of work with that of Addington, who was newly arrived in the work world. She soon arrived at a very simple strategy that worked the first time she tried it: she asked Addington to join her in a quick drink after a particularly tense day. Over drinks they become good friends and their rivalry, while still existing, became an easier and friendlier one.

Eaton's other problem was not so successfully solved. Her other rival was a boy whiz, her age, who had earned partnership in the firm at a prodigiously early age—and who appeared to dislike her on sight for no apparent reason. Her first strategy—discussing their personality conflict with him openly—failed; it was like talking to a brick wall. Once Eaton realized the degree of his inflexibility, she developed a less satisfying but alternate strategy, which was to enlist the aid and support of several other partners whom she subtly made aware of her problem in working with the man. In particular, she told one very senior partner of the constant stream of criticism she was receiving and asked the senior partner if he would give her a progress report from time to time so she would know where her real strengths and weaknesses lay. She got the supportive feedback she needed and had, to boot, at least a 50–50 chance of garnering some support if a showdown became necessary. In her day-to-day dealings with her rival, she maintained a polite but frosty relationship. This strategy hardly reduced what was a deadly serious rivalry, but it made life in that law firm slightly more bearable for everyone involved.

Handling overt and possibly malicious rivals requires a great deal of flexibility. On one level, you must show yourself to be an equally tough competitor—as Eaton did when she enlisted the aid a partner with even more clout than her major rival had—and on another .evel, you have to handle the situation tactfully—again, as Eaton did by maintaining her veneer of good manners even though she was not receiving the same courtesy in return.

Dealing with Others' Underhandedness

Never hesitate to rebuff someone if necessary, particularly someone who will eventually attempt to discredit you openly. If you show initial toughness, your rival may just give up and go on to easier prey.

Attacks by this kind of rival often take the form of a challenge, particularly when you are both in an important meeting. It may also take the form of criticism intended to shake your confidence.

If the criticism or challenge is public, change the battlefield to a more private one if at all possible. Stay calm, stay polite, and whatever you do, don't let the issue blow up. You might, for example, respond to a critical statement made during a meeting by saying, "That's an interesting point, Bill. Perhaps we should discuss it after the meeting." If your rival continues the attack, he or she will only appear hostile and may even run the risk of raising others' ire by prolonging the meeting, a real *faux pas* in most companies.

Avoid riling this kind of a competitor (or anyone, for that matter) with such statements as: "You're dead wrong about that," or "You don't know what you are talking about." Such statements are arrogant and guaranteed to produce anger in anyone toward whom they are directed. It is, on the other hand, polite and slightly unnerving to a rival to say, in your most gracious tone, "There are probably some facts about this situation that you don't know, and perhaps you would revise your thinking somewhat if you understood them fully."

If a challenger won't quit, you will have no choice but to rebuff him or her. Particularly in public, take care to do this in polite, articulate, measured tones that show you mean business. To withdraw at such a time, either in anger or with perfect grace, is liable to be taken as a sign of weakness on your part—not a good executive quality.

A dash of polite anger can even, on occasion, be put to work for you. Show anger, if you must, but do not let it disintegrate into rage. Most important, reserve displays of anger for moments when they will be truly effective; anger is not worth wasting on small things that do not matter to you.

When you must make a counterattack that shows a degree of anger, try to do it privately. Do not do it, however, over dinner or drinks; the issue is a professional matter and should be transacted in your office if at all possible.

Tell your rival you want to speak with him or her. Begin the confrontation by pointing out that you have been angered by the unfairness of the person's actions. If he or she reiterates your errors again, be prepared to defend yourself, if necessary, to show that you know your strengths, but do not let the conversation sink to a nitpicking level. The point in showing anger during a confrontation with a rival is to warn the person off, not to extend the battle over what either of you thinks is right or wrong. State flatly that you will not tolerate unfair or untrue comments, particularly when they are made in public places, such as in a conference with your bosses. Be specific about what you will not tolerate. Do not add any "or elses." Let the other person worry about what they may be. Try to be the one to end the conversation.

The next time you see your rival, be polite, although this is not the time to gush or extend an olive branch that might be taken as a sign of weakness. Such an action could, in fact, undermine the element of threat in your previous meeting. A rival will undoubtedly be prepared for further hostility on your part and may likely be harboring some, so a show of good manners will serve to throw him or her further off balance and possibly make others wonder what the person's new level of hostility toward you is all about.

Overcoming Malicious Gossip

Gossip is part of any office's informal channel of communication. There is one wise way to participate: earn a reputation for not gossiping and keep alert to any gossip that is interesting or helpful to you. If someone is spreading malicious or damaging rumors about you, you will want to know about it, and one way of ensuring that you will hear about it is to be receptive to it.

Rumors may seem to be too petty a subject even to bother with but, sadly, more than one career has been needlessly destroyed by a wily competitor who was all too willing to stoop to them. Beware—and be prepared. The most damaging kinds of rumors are those that have to do with sex and how you do your work. A rival may also start a rumor that you are actively seeking another job or even that you have accepted one.

When a damaging rumor is started, confront its originator as soon as possible—in public. Since you are going to handle this situation in a calm, polite, up-front manner, and since there is little doubt about the motives of the person who has started the gossip, you have nothing to lose and everything to gain by making the confrontation a public one.

Even if the rumor contains a grain of truth, all is not lost. You still may be able to outwit a rival while not obviously denying the rumor. A well-mannered public confrontation might go like this:

J.:   I understand that you have been telling people that I am having an affair with Jane in accounting.

M.:   (*probably in a very flustered voice*) Well, I did hear something to that effect.

J.:   And so you passed it on to a few people.

M.:   (*very flustered*) I don't remember, I may have told someone.

J.:   Where exactly did you hear this?

M.:   Why, ah, Betty, the woman I ride home with, told me she heard it from someone in accounting.

J.:   Well, I would really like to get to the bottom of this, so suppose you and I go talk with Betty to find out more about it.

Sometimes you don't even have to go this far to confront someone who has spread a rumor about you. You might simply say:

K.:   I heard that you told our boss that I was planning to accept a new position with ABC Corporation.

S.:   *(will probably just stutter)*

K.:   Well, that's quite a piece of misinformation, isn't it?

S.:   *(more stuttering, or)* I don't know. Is it?

K.:   It certainly is. I've straightened it out with our boss, and I assume that you won't be repeating it anymore.

End of exchange and end of rumor, most likely. What is interesting about this exchange is that K. just might have been making a move to accept a new position. But if he or she does not yet know for sure that the new position will materialize, or even if it will be accepted if it does, then K. can honestly label the rumor as misinformation. And even if K. cannot honestly so label it, it might be better to do so anyway for the sake of self-preservation.

Mending Fences

Fortunately, there are not a lot of infighters who will go for the jugular in the ways we have just been discussing. Most instances of competitiveness are small flare-ups that may momentarily irritate you but not truly anger or jeopardize you professionally. Therefore, whenever possible, let meaningless gossip or malicious acts go past you. Always try to save ammunition for the big fights. And finally, it is just good manners always to be willing to make an ally of a former rival. It is better for you, your colleagues, and the morale of the company if you maintain an optimistic, open stance. Locking horns with someone once doesn't mean you're destined to be a lifelong enemy. In fact, someone who thinks enough of you to make you a serious rival might do wonders working on your behalf. Always look for a chance to mend fences whenever you have had a run-in with a colleague—over lunch or with drinks after work, or work out your aggressions on the racquetball court.

Finding Friends and Allies

Finding friends among peers can be almost as difficult as pacifying rivals. If true friendships don't appear to be accessible, as is often the case, at least look for alliances. You will need a *côterie* of peers to play your executive skills off against—and if you are a good friend to others, they will invariably return the favor.

Start by earning a reputation for loyalty. This will make you attractive as an ally or a friend, and others will be anxious to work with you. While it may, as a last resort, be necessary to go after a rival who threatens your position, *never* betray a friend.

Underlying even the best friendship or work alliance is a sense of competition. A friend made at work, however close he or she may appear to be, is rarely as close as a childhood friend or old college roommate. After all, you both have an identical goal—advancing your careers.

Persons often comment that they became good friends with a colleague only after one of them moved to another company, a statement that contains more than a kernel of sound advice: Do not let yourself get too involved in the personal life of a coworker. If that person's life takes a bad turn or he or she heads into a seriously self-destructive pattern, you may have to dissociate yourself as a means of self-preservation.

Dissociating yourself from someone bent on doing himself or herself in, however, does not mean you must relinquish your sense of loyalty. Whatever you do, do not participate in a conspiracy against a coworker, friend or foe. Conspiracies are often all too transparent to bosses, and you will still have to coexist with the conspirators when the coup is finished. It is a good way to earn a label for untrustworthiness in the eyes of others who were wise enough not to participate.

Learning the Importance of the Right Friends

If you are a young executive or a new employee in a company and seeking to make your reputation, it is important to choose friends at work with great care. This does not mean selecting friends only for what they can do for you, nor does it necessarily mean choosing those persons whom you would most enjoy socially. It does mean associating yourself with those of your peers who are earning reputations for themselves as serious, earnest comers within the company.

Frequently, there will be a social group within a company; members will fraternize with each other during the day (often to the detriment of their work) and they may see a lot of each other outside work. This group may or may not consist of the real comers in the company; often, particularly if they are young, members are more involved in their social lives than in their professional lives. Groups like this are most often formed by young executives just out of school who miss the informal camaraderie of their school days and want to continue it in an office atmosphere. If you want to make an impression on the top brass, it is better not to be too closely associated with these social groups.

On the other hand, it is always wise to maintain good relations with all your peers. One way to be friends with such a group is to plan to socialize with them occasionally outside work and still maintain a safe distance. Do this by occasionally participating in fairly structured activities—dinner or a round of golf or tennis.

Building Allies

As important as genuine friends are at work, it is also important to have allies—those business associates with whom you see eye to eye and with whom you can strike mutual agreements to help each other from time to time, either in terms of actual time spent working together on a project or in less defined ways, such as supporting each other's ideas in a meeting or speaking well of each other when the opportunity arises. Allies and friends are not necessarily the same thing. As relationships go, alliances are fairly subtle, and there may be no discussion at all about such a tie. But if you have performed a favor for someone, you can expect that he or she will repay you when possible—and vice versa.

Helping Out a Colleague

It is considerate to offer help to a troubled or overworked colleague. Offer one of your workers if a colleague needs extra hands on a project or offer to help out yourself with some important planning that needs to be done in a short amount of time. Whatever you do, do not become a do-gooder about offering your services. Offer only when necessary, and keep your assistance quiet. If the colleague you have helped is at all knowledgeable about the etiquette of business, he or she will give you due credit at an appropriate moment or make sure word of your generosity gets around.

Handling Your Promotion

Sometimes office relationships are temporarily thrown off balance when one member of a peer group is promoted. Graciousness to those who were not promoted this time around can help to ease the situation. Be ready with little amenities—extra praise, help on a project—to soothe any wounded feelings. Take the initiative by asking your previous peers to lunch or to some other social activity. As you move up the ranks ahead of peers, the friendships may indeed change, but you can at least ease the transition by your gracious consideration of others.

MANAGING RELATIONSHIPS WITH A SECRETARY

A few years ago, office etiquette was far more formal. Even after working together for twenty years, a secretary and boss used "Mr.," "Miss," or "Mrs." and surnames with each other. Today, office life is far more informal—and harder to keep under control. First names are frequently used throughout a company—the only one who seems to be able to command the respect of "Mr." or "Ms." these days is the company president or chairperson of the board, and even he or she does not always manage to do so. Such informality is not a cause for complaint; after all, coworkers spend eight or more hours a day together year after year. In retrospect, it seems ridiculous that persons could be so closely associated with one another for so long and maintain so much formality.

A boss is the one to make the decision whether or not to call a secretary by his or her first name; just keep in mind that if you decide to do so, he or she may well respond by calling you by your first name.

Since you will see your secretary frequently throughout the day, there is no need to rise when he or she comes into the room. It is polite to gesture for a secretary to sit down whenever he or she has obviously come in to talk with you at any length, particularly if your working relationship is new and your secretary is not sure what to expect from you.

Bosses today do take their secretaries for lunch—and these are not necessarily working lunches. It is simply a gracious gesture to ask a secretary or assistant—or any other subordinate, for that matter—to be your guest at lunch on occasion. Birthdays and secretaries' appreciation days offer excellent opportunities to show your appreciation in this way.

When appropriate, introduce a secretary or assistant to visitors to the office. If you are in conference with a client, and your secretary brings you sandwiches or coffee, for example, it is only gracious to make introductions when you thank him or her.

A good rule of thumb when making the introduction is to use whatever form of the names you think the persons involved will use later. For example, if a very senior and older executive is in your office, it is only gracious to say: "Mr. Riley, I would like you to meet Ms. Baden, my secretary." If the person in your office is a peer and your office is informal about using first names, you could say: "Bob Jones, I'd like you to meet Sandra Locke."

Take care not to monopolize a secretary's time. It is a secretary's right to have lunch with whomever he or she pleases, so while an occasional working lunch may be acceptable, asking for working lunches on a regular basis is rude. The same thing applies to asking a secretary to work overtime; it may occasionally be necessary, but to do so on a regular basis infringes on his or her privacy. If a great deal of overtime is expected, say, at particular times of the year, this is something you should discuss when you are describing the job to a potential employee.

Above all, show respect for the work a secretary or assistant does for you. Secretaries' work is important and in many ways eases your work load. Although secretaries today have become vocal about their demands, a good boss can do a lot to ease relationships by offering fair and gracious treatment before it is demanded.

Any number of important and not so important tasks belong to a secretary or assistant. He or she will handle your correspondence, book appointments, make travel plans, do filing and typing, and carry messages and memos to others; a bright secretary may correct your spelling or do some slight editing of an obviously ungrammatical sentence. He or she should not be expected to wait on you or perform personal services. Personal services include such chores as bringing coffee (unless the secretary is going to get some for himself or herself or you are in an important meeting with someone), balancing your checkbook, or lying about your whereabouts. Your secretary may, of course, answer your phone, and he or she may well protect you from unwanted callers by saying that you can't take a call or are in conference. Just do not ask him or her to tell obvious lies, particularly those that relate to your private life.

MANAGING RELATIONSHIPS WITH SUPERIORS

The tone of relationships with bosses and others in top management are set by them. They may see their junior executives socially—over dinner, lunch, or drinks or for a round of golf or tennis at the country club—but they will probably not be seeking an intimate friendship.

Since top management is what you want to be part of, it is wise to handle yourself as if you already were part of it. For example, never refer to or even start thinking of superiors as "they." Try to look and think as if you were one. If your superiors work long, hard hours, take a clue that this will be expected of you if you want to advance. Note the way bosses dress, and pattern your dress accordingly (see Chapters 10 and 11). Take note of the amount of formality and informality in the office from what the bosses do, as opposed to what your peers do—if the bosses work in rolled-up shirt sleeves, you can probably do the same; if they do not, you should avoid doing it.

USING MANNERS TO HANDLE YOUR BOSS

Just as it is worth paying attention to the psychological motivations of coworkers, it is also important to sense a boss's ego needs. On the other hand, there is no reason to pander. If the boss is good at what he or she does, he or she will not be particularly interested in having a *côterie* of yes-people around. Departing from the boss's views—if done politely and without hostility—only shows that you have the qualities of leadership. Besides, trying to please everyone makes you look weak and ineffectual, and even the largest ego knows when it is being played like a musical instrument. On the other hand, it is important to sense a boss's ego needs and defer in those areas where the boss seems to need it.

Always play straight with a boss when reviewing your work. The boss is the person who will or will not go to bat for you and so has a right to know whether you are running late or having any special problems with work. Also, never promise more than you can deliver. As persons achieve greater success, they become less likely to jump at taking on new responsibilities, so while it is important to take on whatever you can handle to get ahead, you won't win anyone's respect if you overestimate what you can actually accomplish.

HANDLING CONFIDENTIAL INFORMATION

Finally, while discretion is important in all phases of business, it is never more so than when a boss shares a confidence with you. As you move up in the company, you will be privy to increasingly important information. Learn to keep confidential information quiet. Some bosses interviewed even admitted to "setting up" an employee as a means of testing how well he or she would be able to keep important confidences. So beware the tidbit that seems too unimportant to keep secret even though you have been requested to do so. Besides, it is simply good manners to keep confidential anything that someone indicates is private.

TAKING CRITICISM GRACIOUSLY

It is also important to learn to accept criticism from superiors graciously. First, never lose your poise when criticized. Do not offer excuses, and above all, do not take the criticism personally. It is only intended to help. Thank the person who offers criticism. One very wise executive said he always counters with: "Is there anything else I should know that would help me in my work?" It is a mistake to meet criticism with a flip response, a joke, laughter, and most certainly, with a defensive or sharp reply. These are rude ways to treat anyone who is trying to help you.

HANDLING SUBORDINATES WHEN YOU HAVE JUST BECOME THE BOSS

Abrasive managers do occasionally succeed, but they are the

exceptions, and rarely do they command loyalty from the persons they work with. Try to treat those who work for you with graciousness and to respect their work. Never underestimate the power of a subordinate—even the least important filing clerk—to sabotage your work if disgruntled.

Many executives who are first given responsibility for other employees are unsure of the etiquette of working with their new subordinates. For starters, do not expect too much. This isn't a personality contest. Be friendly, but do not be a pal. Intimacy and friendliness are not the same thing; with the former you may find yourself leaned upon in a way that can be detrimental to your ambition.

Remember that a truly good leader motivates others to do their best. As a new boss, you might begin by asking your employees for written job descriptions. This will help you analyze how they see themselves and to plan a corresponding strategy for treating them.

Be open with those who work for you. Explain what you will and will not tolerate and also explain decisions about work that will affect them. Leave subordinates room to differ with you, but remember that you are the boss and that you must eventually be the one to make the decisions.

Sooner or later, you will have to handle a dispute among subordinates. There is an art to doing this. First, do not play favorites. Insist that the feuding employees treat each other politely and with respect; then treat both of them with respect in turn. One good ploy is to ask each person for written memos detailing the aspects of the dispute. This will give you some breathing room and will force the arguing persons to confront the issue more directly.

MAINTAINING PRIVACY

Now that you have learned how to promote goodwill among

your colleagues, it may be necessary to learn how to avoid colleagues tactfully when you have important things to do. One sign of a good executive is the ability to manage time well. The Harvard Business School, is rumored to routinely assign its students more reading than they can possibly handle as a means of teaching them to be selective about their reading—just as a good executive must be selective about using his or her time.

Some of the tips that follow are matters of etiquette (how to discourage a pest from talking too long), and others are simply tips on how to get the time you need.

Every office has its yakker; someone really should estimate how many millions of dollars are lost every year to routine but unnecessary office chitchat. When you are cornered by one of these persons, the way you handle the situation depends upon the rank of the person. If your boss likes to come in to talk at length, obviously you tolerate it, work late to compensate—and get another job if the problem becomes serious. Rarely, though, will an excessive talker be a top power; executives do not get to the top by wasting time—a fact to keep in mind. If it is a colleague who is overstaying his or her welcome, start fidgeting with the papers on your desk or cast wistful looks at your piles of work. If this doesn't work, say firmly: "What you are saying is very interesting, and I wish I could talk about it longer, but I am feeling pressure to finish this memo I'm preparing." Another technique is to stand up, put an arm around the pest, and walk him or her out of your office. If the person still doesn't take the hint, you are stuck—unless you want to be rude, which isn't a bad idea if someone is too boorish to know when to leave. Finally, a sure way to get rid of someone is to get up and leave the room yourself.

A subordinate who talks too much—to you or to anyone else—can be reined in by a polite but firm talk about not wasting time in the office.

As for guarding your time for important work, the first step is to rank work according to its urgency. One very successful executive reported that for years she had done only the urgent work and that no one had ever pressed her for any other work. Another executive reported that he escaped to an unused office or a conference room when he had pressing work to do. Several executives reported having their calls held or even limiting them to one specific time of day. One junior executive kept a small timer on his desk and tried not to spend over five minutes on any phone call.

The important thing to remember in office relationships is to treat others with the same respect you would like to receive. Assume that all kinds of work are important, as indeed they are. Earn a reputation for polite, fair dealings with all your coworkers, and you will find yourself rewarded immensely at appropriate moments—moments that can be crucial to your career.

CHAPTER 2

Sex in the Office
and
Other Tricky Relationships

N O MATTER what the official line is, sex has always been part of the office scene. Since the sexual revolution and the women's rights movement, which have brought more women into offices in professional capacities, office relationships have taken an entirely new turn. While a female secretary or clerical worker may think twice about putting a job in jeopardy by indulging in an office affair, women who work as peers with men have less to lose.

Some women have even gained enough power to turn the tables and go after men in whom they are interested. Since some men have been playing this game for years, this is really just a new twist on an old power play. Men who are the subjects of sexual approaches from women will have to learn to handle them as tactfully as women have tried to do over the years.

USING DISCRETION—THE KEY TO PLAYING AROUND IN THE OFFICE

Philosophical discussion aside, handling an office affair does require some discretion. Moreover, what two persons can get away with is directly related to the moral attitudes of the boss or management.

If you have a boss who is casual about sexual relationships or about personal friendships at work, you will probably encounter little resistance to an office affair. If you have a straitlaced boss, resistance may be so high that you will find you must keep an affair under wraps. Such feelings vary widely—some bosses, for example, object to married persons' playing around but are more tolerant of affairs between single employees. Other bosses indulge in such activity themselves and would hardly have cause to say anything to another employee.

Total indiscretion is about the only thing you cannot get away with. Being caught *in flagrante delicto* in the office can and probably will get you fired. One young Wall Street lawyer finally managed (on a Saturday afternoon) to indulge his fantasy of putting the board room to his idea of good use only to discover that his activities led directly to his being fired a few weeks later.

While it seems that you can often get away with an office affair, most bosses and coworkers are justifiably irked at public displays of affection—long conversations during work, lunch taken for too long and at irregular hours for what might be deemed irregular purposes, and in some offices, lovers' being indiscreet enough to walk in together in the morning. (For more on how to conduct an office affair, see page 35.)

In other offices, however, where two persons are known to be having a relationship or even living together, bosses and coworkers think it is silly for them not to walk in together if they have in fact spent the night together.

Most bosses draw the line when a personal relationship interferes with work. A relationship has gotten out of hand when it starts to interfere with the work of one or another of the pair—through either overt exchanges of loving looks or the lovers' spats that occur at work.

The amount of discretion necessary for interoffice relationships can vary within a single office from year to year. One astute observer of a publishing firm that had seen more than its share of office romances in the past few years, most of which had culminated in a flurry of divorces, marriages, and cohabitation relationships, noted, "A year ago when office romances were the big thing, there was a lot of sexual talk in the office during the day. The talk was split between those who dropped hints about their own sexual lives and those who dropped comments about the sexual lives of others. At the moment, there are no office romances going on—at least, none that I know about—and there is almost no sexual banter, either. The subject of sex just never comes up during working hours anymore. And although there has been no change in top management, I think everyone senses that playing around obviously with someone in the office would not be accepted very readily today. For some strange reason, the mood is straighter now."

ASKING THE BOSS TO DINNER WHEN YOU COHABIT

In these days of cohabitation, the question of whether or not to have the boss to dinner—and expose your personal life—often arises. Again, a boss's reaction to this situation is likely to be highly personal. Some bosses have no second thoughts about socializing with an employee who is unmarried and living with someone, while other bosses do not want to know anything about your living habits. You have to take a reading on your boss and decide how open you can be.

The answer, if you have a live-in roommate, is not to invite the boss to dinner with the idea that the boss had better accept your values . . . or else. If you are friends with your boss out of work, however, chances are he or she is aware of your life style and has no complaints. You can feel free to socialize without hiding anything.

If you do not socialize with your boss, and you sense that your actions would only earn disapproval, do not invite the boss to dinner—or do anything so overt that the boss will have to face the fact that you are living with someone. At company parties or on other social occasions, take your friend if you are invited to bring someone, but do not make an obvious point of letting people know you are roommates unless you are sure it won't matter.

If you know that the place where you work is generally stuffy, your best bet is to be discreet about your relationship with all your coworkers and not just the boss. Being discreet, unfortunately, often means telling white lies about the nature of the relationship and the living arrangements. While no one enjoys having to lie about so major a part of one's life, remember that your career is also a major part of your life—and that you want to control the direction it takes. The white lie is usually worth it if you sense that you will meet with severe disapproval.

Such a white lie is usually successful, since the people in this kind of office are less likely to fraternize with one another than those who work in more easygoing offices.

HANDLING SEXUAL BANTER IN THE OFFICE

In many offices a certain amount of sexual banter is part of the daily routine. After all, these are adult human beings with whom you spend a large chunk of time every day year after year. Never to discuss sex—either directly or indirectly—would be highly artificial.

Sexual banter in an office is no more serious than any other kind of light joking about any other subject, and in many instances, responding the right way to a light pass can help you ward off a more serious pass.

One professional woman who works with many lawyers has developed her own method of dealing with sexual banter and the occasional serious pass. If someone with less-than-innocent motives asks, "How about a drink after work?" she replies, "Actually, I've wanted you for a long time. Why don't you leave your wife and run away with me?" She continues in this vein until the other person realizes he won't be taken seriously and goes away. She swears her technique has kept her out of serious trouble. In part she gets away with her outrageous comments because she has a reputation for no nonsense in the office about work or personal matters and, in part, because her banter calls the other person's bluff.

SAYING NO

Occasionally the sexual banter does turn into a serious pass. This can happen to men and women, and each individual must decide how to handle the situation.

If you find the person attractive and want to follow up on the relationship, that is fine. You are on your own, since this section deals with how to say no and minimize the damage to your career and another person's ego.

Usually signals are sent back and forth before a serious overture is made, and if you are not interested, this is the time to drop hints to that effect. The easiest way to ward off a pass is to be busy with someone else who occupies a lot of your free time outside work. When you sense that an overture is in the offing, that is the time to start making regular mention of "the person I go with."

If the situation is still fairly light, and you sense that this is a serious but nonmanipulative pass, you can be more relaxed about it. You might even say, "You know, I really do find you attractive, but I'm seriously involved with someone at the moment" or the more honest, "I do think you're attractive and I'm flattered, but I just don't get involved with the people I work with."

One man reported that dropping hints of an earlier and very sad and unsuccessful office relationship—in another office, of course—was enough to cool things off.

If you know you are not willing to put up with anything sexual that involves a coworker, be ready with a firm statement about your feelings. There is, however, no reason to snarl or unnecessarily hurt another person, so smile and use a pleasant voice. One stockbroker reported stopping all suggestions for office romance dead by saying without a smile, "I'm sorry, but I am just not interested in that. I know you will understand." If badgered, she repeated her message and left the room as soon as possible.

A man or woman need have only one reservation about using the "I'm sorry, I don't do that with my coworkers" excuse, and that is that someday you might find you *want* to become involved with a coworker, which could cause bitter feelings on the part of the person you turned down earlier. Of course, it would be rude of him or her to remind you of this, but you may find it is easier in the long run not to use this excuse unless you mean it.

The newest etiquette problem on the sexual scene at work is pressure from women on men. Men who are feeling pressure to socialize with or even to romance a female boss can use tact and graciousness to ease an awkward situation. Try to turn the person down with a compliment—if you want to do so. Say you are too involved with another person at this time—in short, act flattered, flatter the other person, but firmly say no.

DEALING WITH SEXUAL HARASSMENT

Executives rarely use techniques of harassment among each other, but occasionally a person will find himself or herself in such a bind. This is not a time to be polite. If the harassment is truly severe, and you feel you cannot control it yourself, go to the boss of the person who is harassing you. Most such complaints are taken very seriously these days.

About the only etiquette involved in doing this, and it is merely a last-ditch attempt to save face for all involved, is to warn the person politely that if you are not left alone, you will talk to someone with the power to do something to stop the harassment.

FORMING MENTOR FRIENDSHIPS

For years men have had mentors who promoted their careers, and this has never been cause for comment. But since women have achieved a measure of power, more and more women are finding that they must cope with the ramifications of maintaining a close and often platonic relationship with a boss-mentor or an older, more powerful executive who has taken a personal interest in her career. And some young men are finding themselves with female mentors.

In some offices, these relationships are accepted and there is no cause for comment from one's coworkers. In other offices, such a relationship may be mistaken for an office romance or may cause resentments among coworkers who misunderstand the nature of the relationship, or who understand it perfectly and still resent it.

About the best you can do with this situation is to weather it through. Obviously, a mentor relationship is beneficial to anyone's career and is not something to be dismissed lightly. You can play down the relationship and take care not to flaunt it among your peers. Try to ignore any particularly gossipy comments, although one good thing about this kind of gossip is that it rarely reaches the ears of the person who is its subject. If you work in an office where your relationship is resented, no one will believe your denials anyway, so it is best to say nothing and be as discreet as possible about the relationship.

FORMING PEER FRIENDSHIPS

Friendships among coworkers often are struck up these days, since men and women work together in positions of equality and, in many cases, travel together. How peer friendships are handled is a personal decision on the part of those involved.

If you work in a very straight office, there is no point in adding grist to the gossip mill. If you enjoy a coworker's company and a friendship develops, skip the long lunches or other activities that normally give rise to gossip in the office, and meet after work—unless, of course, you do not care and you are sure the gossips will not be able to harm your career.

There is no particular reason to explain such a relationship, even if one or both friends are married to other persons. Simply enjoy the friendship as discreetly as possible and say little to anyone about it.

MAINTAINING AN OFFICE ROMANCE

Frequently two persons meet at work and discover that they genuinely care for each other. Of the executives interviewed, no one condemned this kind of relationship as long as it was handled with discretion. There are, however, a few things that two persons involved in an intense personal relationship can do to ease their work situation.

First, don't flaunt it. Coworkers and top brass alike will be more tolerant of the relationship if they are not made to feel awkward over it. Longing looks or lovers' spats, even insiders' comments that have meaning only to the two of you, are best avoided.

It is a matter of courtesy to make an extra effort to be discreet when you are at work, and the less you bring your personal relationship to work, the less chance that it will harm your career.

Two lovers may find that they work better when they are separated. In that case, there is no reason why one of you cannot request a transfer to another department of a large company. If one of you decides to seek another job outside the company, that is another matter that should be conducted as discreetly and quietly as any job hunt would be.

HANDLING THE END OF AN AFFAIR

Occasionally an office romance will go sour and, just as often, an outside romance or marriage will break up and you will find that your personal life weighs heavily on your professional life.

However torn up you may be, your coworkers are not necessarily the people who should have to bear the brunt of your pain. It is neither professional nor polite to bring such problems to work. If life is really unbearable, take a few days off—and give a reason other than a broken heart unless you know you have a very understanding boss.

If you must continue working with an ex-lover, try to be civil, at least during the times you spend around others. Spare coworkers the gory details, if at all possible, and above all, don't take pot shots at your ex-lover. This is not for his or her sake, but for yours. Unrequited love only makes everyone feel ill at ease, and people may well start to avoid you just at a time when you need them most.

If your ex-lover takes shots at you, your best bet is to ignore them. Most persons will see what is going on and also observe your good behavior.

The etiquette of office romances varies from office to office. Status symbols in one company, they can contribute to one's demise in another. The key to the amount of discretion required during such a relationship is your boss. If you value your career, you simply have to take a reading on his or her feelings and act accordingly. And remember that no one has ever been accused of using too much discretion when having an office romance.

CHAPTER 3

The Etiquette of Handling Your Boss

THE MOST IMPORTANT RELATIONSHIP you must develop—and you must develop it in every single job you ever have—is with your boss. And make no mistake about it, *you* must be the one to nurture and develop the relationship. A boss has the power to hire and fire and does not have to mend his or her ways to fit the attitudes and values of employees. You, on the other hand, have to make an extra effort to work with the boss or be prepared to end up on the street.

Peter F. Drucker, a fountain of wisdom on boss-employee relations, has pointed out in his books that overrating a superior carries no stigma. You win an ally and show loyalty to someone whom you respect. Underrating a boss, on the other hand, can be insulting if he or she is sensitive enough to notice, and can eventually result in your being unable to work together.

From a practical standpoint, you should be doing everything possible to help your boss succeed. The sooner the boss is promoted, the sooner another door is opened to you.

Then, too, the way you handle the relationship with the boss is a matter of concern to everyone in the company. The top brass will be watching your manner, particularly if they know you are working with a notoriously unpleasant person, and developing a working relationship with someone who is known as being tough to get along with does win points in the long run. Boss management tells a lot about anyone's management potential.

UNDERSTANDING YOUR BOSS

Perhaps the best way to begin to understand your boss is to realize that he or she is human, has weaknesses and strengths, and may from time to time be beset with the same financial and personal problems that plague the rest of us.

Realize, too, that you are on this person's team. A boss does not owe an employee anything, whereas an employee owes his or her job to a boss. Therefore, your task is to fit into the boss's working habits, time schedule, and plans and goals for the future.

The rules for getting along with a boss are fairly short and simple. First decide whether you have a reader or a listener. Since a large part of your time must be spent communicating with your boss, it is important to find the best way to do so right off the bat. Readers prefer to get their information in written form—via memos and reports. Try always to give them something to read before going in to talk to them.

Listeners, usually persons who issue statements such as, "My door is always open," and "I always want to talk to you if there is any kind of problem," prefer that you come in directly and chat. They may even find a written communication slightly cold.

Still, appearances can be deceptive. A boss may have read a management book recently that advocated being more accessible to employees when, in fact, he or she still personally prefers little contact and lots of memos and reports. Look under the surface before you type a boss. A boss who says the door is always open but then proceeds to issue two written memos a day is not a boss who truly wants to chat with employees any more than is absolutely necessary. A boss who expresses a desire always to be available to talk with employees but is always rushing off to do something else does not really want this kind of contact. Stick with written memos when you have this kind of boss.

Deciding whether to approach a boss in writing or in person is part of the art of managing the boss's time. While deciding what kind of boss you have, look for clues as to how the boss manages time and then do everything you can to help him use time efficiently. Does the boss like to chat for a few minutes about the day's business just at quitting time? Be willing to hang around and oblige. Does the boss like to be left alone in the morning to work on his or her own projects? Wait until afternoon to confer about your projects.

Another important guideline in getting along with a boss is never to confuse or surprise him or her. In other words, never make your boss appear stupid. Oliver Spencer, president of Graphic Alliance, Inc., a midwestern graphic arts company, commented: "You never want your boss to appear stupid to his boss. He should always have a file, a memo, something— somewhere—on a project you've been working on. This is very important, this face-saving thing. In a big company, especially, nothing is more embarrassing for a boss than to be asked something by the top brass and not even to be aware of what they are talking about."

Keep a boss abreast of your work—the work you are currently handling, as well as the projects that you are going to tackle later and why you have put them off. If a problem arises that is your responsibility, make it known to the boss and discuss your plans for dealing with it.

Along with keeping a boss informed and helping him or her to manage time, always go to the boss's office prepared. You need not have every fact or detail on hand—to do so even could make you appear a bit too detail-oriented—but always be prepared to discuss the topic at hand.

Follow up on all assignments. Bosses who make trivial assignments are often the very ones who remember to ask about them at the most inopportune times, and they rarely forget them entirely.

If a boss has promised to do something for you, remind him or her politely if necessary. Give the boss a chance to do what he or she promises.

Excuses for projects that have gone awry or work that simply has not been done on time can really hurt you. If you sense that you are going to need extra help with a project, discuss this with your boss long before the deadline approaches. If you will require an extension, this, too, should be worked out in advance rather than at the last minute.

THREATENING A BOSS—THE ULTIMATE MISTAKE

A lot of ego is involved in being an executive. The higher one climbs, the less involved one is with actual products and the more involved one is with intangible products, such as the talents and skills of other persons.

It is hard for an up-and-coming executive with some ego involvement of his or her own not to threaten the boss. Yet business survival demands that you not threaten the person you work for. Many young executives could use a course in nonassertiveness training, and some management programs are now offering seminars in this very subject. Assertiveness, which may also be somewhat necessary in the competitive work world, too often looks like arrogance or presumptuousness to the boss or to a conservative, old-school member of the board. Nonassertiveness, on the other hand, is a recognition of the fact that there are situations when a restrained style works best.

Remember that your boss usually will have more information than you will about the company and may or may not be able to share this information with you, and that keeping a relaxed attitude when you sense that you are confronting this situation will do a lot to keep you out of trouble. If your boss suddenly insists that a project be done a certain way, acquiesce.

There are several good nonassertiveness techniques to keep in mind when dealing with a boss. First, remember empathic listening. Give a boss time to tell you about *his* other plans and objectives rather than always pushing yours. Second, develop the skill of delivering facts to your boss in a noncritical way. Occasionally you may be asked to do some research on a touchy project—closing out part of the boss's domain, for example. This is not the time to assert yourself. Instead, just give the boss the facts and let him or her worry about their interpretation. To come up with a finding that makes the boss unhappy, even if you do so innocently, may be threatening.

Third, learn the art of selective passivity. You will do better to remain aloof from some issues. If your boss has been ordered from above to cut back on managers because the company had a bad year, and you have some dynamic new management techniques that could save the situation, this is still not the time to mention them. Again, it just threatens a boss who is losing some power. Try to remain aloof from the situation, as far as your boss is concerned.

If you want to challenge your boss, and there is no reason not to do this occasionally, do it privately. Prepare your argument in advance and make sure it is well thought out. Public power plays with a boss are invariably seen as a threat to the boss's power base, and a smart boss won't let anyone get away with that very many times.

If you sense that, despite efforts to the contrary, you are threatening the boss, some nonassertiveness training or a few sessions with a good counselor may help to work out the kinks of the relationship. Then, too, there are those bosses who just cannot tolerate bright young people; it is best to give up on them and look elsewhere for a job where you can shine. Truly poor managers also should be abandoned, as should bosses who are corrupt, unfair, overly critical, and incompetent, and those who only want yes-people working for them. While you can usually arrive at a compromise working situation with most bosses where such a personality conflict is involved, a young executive is never really allowed to shine in such cases, and it is better to advance your career in another company or another department, if possible.

BEING THE BOSS

The other side of the coin occurs when you, the boss, have responsibility for a number of people. It is sometimes harder, just because of the power that goes along with being the boss, to treat employees in a nonassertive, gracious manner. Yet doing so can lower employee defenses, improve interpersonal relationships, and motivate young executives—in short, it can make everyone on your team pull that much harder for you, and this is what management is all about.

Milton Wood, president of Wood Computer Associates, Inc., a well-known executive placement company, drew on his own experience of running a company and his experience in counseling the numerous executives his company has placed, to comment: "Management is a science in itself. A truthful managerial style develops around an executive's personality. Many executives are poor managers. They are either self-concerned with their own ego and position, or they do not take time to learn to delegate and manage properly. The success or failure of any manager is a direct product of the people he can hire, fire, manage, motivate and retain. If you're the type of man who has to do everything yourself, you're doomed to fail. The hard-nosed SOB-type manager who doesn't develop some type of personal relationship with his key people is also doomed to fail, because it's only through *ésprit de corps* that you can accomplish things. That does not mean you're a divorce counselor or a financial manager or any kind of dumping ground for an employee's emotional problems, but there has to be some kind of relationship where employees feel you are personally concerned with their professional growth."

A good manager of others needs to remember to use the same nonassertiveness techniques that he or she used or uses with his own boss, plus a few other techniques. The art of procrastination has some benefits when you are motivating others, for example. Let employees work out their interpersonal squabbles. As long as no one is getting hurt, let an employee work out a project on his or her own time. Mature adults generally work well by themselves. They don't need a mother hen clucking over them every minute, nor should a boss assume that he or she has a captive audience whenever an employee comes looking for advice or a suggestion. If possible, help someone seeking advice to think through the problem and to find his or her own solution. Above all, when giving advice, avoid the tendency to expound. The boss who constantly expounds on various subjects to his or her employees often knows little about what truly goes on in the office and thus has little control over the persons he or she manages.

EXPRESSING DISSATISFACTION

However much loyalty is owed to a boss, there are times when an executive wants to take on more authority or simply wants the opportunity to shine more within the company than the boss will permit. There are ways to manage this. When you want to express dissatisfaction with a boss over the amount of authority you don't have—or about any other problem, for that matter—try to do so diplomatically. Let your boss know that you are unhappy about something and would like to talk it over as soon as possible. Prepare carefully for the meeting. Go into it with a calm attitude; be very organized and know exactly what you hope to accomplish in the meeting. If you seek more authority, know why it should be given to you and how the company will benefit from it. Wood said: "You get a lot more mileage by selling a function and by trying to understand a boss's reactions—why he is the way he is—and by then trying to work a solution around that than by producing a threatening situation. The person who goes in to see his manager to gripe without having a remedy is wrong. Why is the boss reluctant to give up some of his authority? Was he stung by a subordinate who took advantage of him? If this is the case, try to develop a level of trust so that the boss will give you a shot at what you want to do."

Even if you have to back off the first couple of times you try for more authority rather than threaten a boss, do so. Gradually a bond of trust will build and you will probably get the authority or anything else you seek.

GOING AROUND A BOSS

Sometimes you have no choice but to work around a boss. There is, however, an art to doing this. You can go around your boss to the boss's superiors if you keep your boss fully informed of what you are doing. Write a memo to your boss detailing any contact with a superior. When you have gone around your boss, say so and then add, "I got an OK from (*your boss's boss*) on that," or "(*Your boss's boss*) said to go ahead with the project as soon as possible." Actually, the only time you should go around a boss this way is when you truly believe that the boss is not doing the job as well as it could be done and you are convinced that you can do it better; such bosses usually know they aren't cutting the ice and will rarely give a young executive a fight when he or she starts to work around them. If you are reprimanded for going over the boss's head (and a boss who understands power will not waste a moment in doing this) back off, claim innocence, and don't repeat the offense. You have warned your boss that you need more authority, and he or she will either give it to you or not.

A more subtle way to go around a boss is to get exposure for yourself. A bright young man who worked for a Louisville manufacturer but felt held down by his boss, the division sales manager, came up with the idea of taping sales messages that salespersons could carry around with them and play while they drove from appointment to appointment. He went right over his boss's head to sell the idea, won the recognition he deserved, and eventually went out on his own to sell his product.

Along the same line, you could give slide presentations and talks, organize seminars, or do anything that gets you known around the company. Your boss won't be able to do anything as you direct your energies in new directions, as long as you are still doing the job you were hired to do. And you will be making countless allies and contacts.

COPING WITH TOO MUCH AMBITION

Be careful, however, not to overexpose yourself or get a reputation for being too ambitious. Ambition that is too obvious can hurt. It usually earns one the reputation of being "too hot to handle." Usually such men and women appear to burn out early in their careers. In effect, what happens is that no one will take them on, since no one wants a worker who is so obviously promoting only himself or herself. Even when getting exposure for yourself, it is important to give the appearance that you are doing this for the company's benefit. As one executive at IBM said, "Why should I give a break to a guy who, however bright and talented, weighs every work project in terms of how it will look on his résumé?"

Executives who get too hot to handle rarely get fired; instead, they get a lot of lateral promotions and wake up one day to find themselves on dead-end career paths. This happens most often in large corporations. Here, one does not threaten a boss. There are so many jobs that one can simply be shoved aside or moved from place to place because no one wants to advance the career of someone who is busy advancing himself or herself every minute.

COMPLAINING ABOUT A COLLEAGUE

It is an archaic philosophy to think that you cannot go to a boss to complain if someone with whom you work is not doing his or her job properly, but there is an etiquette to complaining. First, you must know what you can legitimately complain about. As one executive noted, "You can only lose face if you go in to complain because the secretarial pool doesn't get your letters out fast enough." Then, too, it is wiser not to complain about anyone on a level higher than you; it may threaten your boss, who will undoubtedly have his or her own peer loyalties.

Most bosses advise that a person go first to the colleague who is not doing his or her job satisfactorily. Since you still need to work with this person, it is more tactful to try to work things out with him or her before going to the boss. If this fails and you feel you have to go to your boss, you can do it, but as one man noted, "You can complain, but you have to couch the complaint in diplomatic terms. For instance, if you need to work with that colleague, you almost have to go to your boss and suggest another method of getting the job done, one that takes the burden off the person who is not carrying his load. You can't ever go in and bad-mouth a colleague. You really can't gossip, either. You mostly have to go in and describe the work situation to the boss—often without using names—and hope that he gets the message."

Most executives do get the message. They know when they have someone working for them who is not pulling his or her weight, and they take a complaint from a colleague, however subtly it may be worded, as a sign that the time has come for action.

When a general air of dissatisfaction prevails in an office, a direct confrontation with top management often works. It has worked so well at Dean, Witter in Chicago that Thomas Clark, branch office manager, regularly schedules "beer and bitch" sessions at which employees can open up in an informal session with their superiors. Clark said, "Everyone gets a couple of beers in him and then lets off as much steam as he wants to. There's no pressure because we're in a group. There aren't any hard feelings the next day, and I learn a lot." The key to these sessions is their collective nature and the fact that the employees can really open up to their boss. After all, bosses are not mind readers—there are times when they simply have not yet caught the vibrations that all is not well in the offices.

DEALING WITH A BOSS WHO ERRS

Sometimes your superior will make an embarrassing blunder, and you, as the subordinate trying your hardest to advance your career and the boss's, will find that you must react. There are three things you can do tactfully when this happens. First, you can ignore the error if it is minor enough. Second, you can defend it. Do this by pointing out the wisdom of your boss's decision. Pointing out the long-term value of the boss's decision is an especially good tactic. Few persons will remember the mistake when the future finally arrives and the decision has been proven right or wrong, and few people know what will happen in the future anyway, so who can say whether your boss has erred or not if you put the mistake in this light?

Finally, if you feel strongly about a boss's error, you can privately and tactfully express your views to the boss. If you feel that the error could harm your career, express your dissatisfaction in a memo for the boss's eyes only—and keep a copy for future reference.

GIVING CRITICISM

One of the functions of being a boss is to critically evaluate the work of your employees. Some companies have procedures for critical evaluation while other companies let each executive handle this in his or her own way. All executives interviewed felt that it was essential to talk over an employee's performance from time to time. Doing so, however, calls for a great deal of tact and graciousness on the part of the person proffering the criticism.

Milton Wood expressed his philosophy on evaluating people this way: "You do have to be tactful, but a boss does an individual a big injustice by not exposing specifically what problems exist. For example, if someone who worked for me didn't speak well, it would be my responsibility to let that person know right up front. I try to tell the person that I want him or her to succeed and that I am confident that he or she will, but that there are a few factors that are not necessarily hurting at the moment, but which should be remedied if the person wants to grow with this organization or professionally. I always try to be diplomatic and I always try to have a solution. A person who doesn't speak well, for example, is offered the opportunity to take a course—at company expense— to improve his or her speech. I also try to sell the reason that the person needs to improve. Most important, I think, is to offer a solution whenever criticism is offered. It makes the criticism seem less ominous."

People work well only when they think they are good at what they do, and to undermine confidence is also to undermine the company, so criticism always should be couched in the most tactful terms. One way to do this is to minimize your authority when giving criticism. Let an employee know that you want to talk about his or her work and ask the person to prepare any notes or thoughts he or she may have. Evaluative sessions should always be a two-way street. If possible, get out from behind your desk when giving criticism and sit in a chair beside the employee or across a table. Let the employee begin. Ask, "How do you think things are going? Do you have any specific problems?"

Focus on just one or two issues and save anything else for another meeting. One executive said, "Not only does a boss have to be diplomatic in giving criticism, but also he has to understand that people aren't perfect. Don't take people to task for something that doesn't amount to a hill of beans. Ignore the minor stuff and go on to the major problems."

Listen very carefully to any complaints an employee has, and avoid giving the impression that you are biding your time until he or she gets done speaking so you can get down to the real business at hand: criticism. When you do get down to specific areas that could be improved, it is important to phrase comments in plain language. One executive reported that a friend at a major oil company had been told he needed to work on motivating those who worked for him, but the suggestion was written in pure corporate jargon, so the person just laughed it off. The executive said, "I could tell that this was a problem with my friend and that, had the suggestion been put to him plainly, he would have responded. But as it was, he entirely missed the point because he found the corporate jargon so funny, and in a way, I could see his point, too."

Major corporations usually have forms that are used in employee evaluation. One oil company executive said he knows just what to do with the forms. He begins every employee-evaluation interview by tearing up the forms and saying, "These don't matter to me. What I want to do is discuss with you seriously what you are doing well and what areas need improvement." He continued, "The employee always responds and we have a good, open talk. Of course, I have to go back later and fill in the forms, but the employee doesn't have to submit to this grading process. Unless something is really wrong with an employee, everyone gets good ratings on those forms, anyway."

Wrap up a critical session by soliciting the employee's goals for the future, by outlining his or her accomplishments, and by discussing what he or she will be doing on current projects. Reassure employees that you value their work and always try to end the session by complimenting an employee on a strong point.

ACCEPTING CRITICISM

No one loves to hear criticism, but everyone wants reinforcement for a job well done. In most companies, one comes with the other, or at least, you cannot escape hearing an evaluation of your work. How you respond to criticism depends in part on the personality of the person giving it and on your relationship with him or her. Never laugh off criticism—always treat it very seriously. Ask for specific examples of situations you have handled poorly. Ask for your boss's ideas on how you might better handle yourself.

When the session is drawing to a close, tell your boss that you appreciate his or her honesty and suggestions. Thank the boss for giving you such a fair report if, in fact, you got one.

Should you find yourself constantly subjected to what you feel is unfair criticism, it may be time to look for another job. You may need a lower-key job or a better boss. In either case, accept the criticism graciously while you work your way to another job or department. Don't give a former boss a chance to tell a prospective boss that you don't take criticism well.

ACCEPTING PUBLIC CRITICISM

Criticism should be given privately. Offering public criticism is invariably an underhanded power play. If someone suggests a truly rotten idea, it will fall of its own accord without another person's cynical prompting. Avoid such demeaning actions.

Should you find yourself being criticized publicly, stay calm—and stay polite. Attention, fairly or not, has been focused on you, and everyone will be watching to see how you handle the situation. Say as little as possible and treat the person who offers the criticism civilly. You could say something vague such as "You may be right," or you could offer to discuss the matter later.

ASKING FOR A PROMOTION OR RAISE

Asking for a promotion or a raise is torture for the timid and downright hard work even for the assertive. Most managers feel that a good employee should not have to ask for a raise, that it should be offered before the employee has a chance to ask for it.

Ironically, there are times when asking for a raise before it is offered is good strategy. Sometimes the biggest raises go to the persons who dare to ask for them. If, for example, the rumor is circulating that raises will be held to 5 percent for management, and you feel that you have done outstanding work, it's appropriate for you to talk with your boss about your work and the fact that you would like a raise of 15 percent for your efforts. Usually a compromise will be achieved—the boss won't be able to get the 15 percent for you, but because you have made it known tactfully that you won't be happy with 5 percent, the boss may fight for you and probably win slightly more than the 5 percent that everyone who doesn't speak up will be getting.

On the other hand, if you know your boss's hands are tied, you can still let it be known that you feel you deserve a raise, but don't take a hard line about something that the boss can't control. To do so only creates unnecessary tension. Giving someone a raise makes a boss feel powerful, but stressing someone's inability to give a raise at a certain time can be threatening.

When Not To Ask For A Raise

Some moments are poor ones for requesting a raise. Even a star employee is unlikely to get a big boost in salary if he or she asks at the end of the company's fiscal year during a year when profits are down. Then, too, if business is in a slump, large raises might be less readily granted.

How to Build Your Case

The only way to ask for a raise is to build a case for why you should be given one. This case, if at all possible, should be built in round dollar figures. Point out the profits of your department or how it has grown over the last year; show how you have contributed to the company's growth. Never ask for a raise because you need the money personally or because you have just bought a new house or car and must make payments.

Raises and promotions are almost never based on performance charts but are instead based on personal evaluation. Even a company that appears to have a tight salary schedule is almost always more flexible than you would imagine, so never let this stop you from asking for whatever amount you think you are worth, which in most companies in relatively good economic times is about 15 percent above your present salary. Even if you are sure raises are set in the company you work for, see your boss and let him or her know that you want more before the boss meets with superiors to determine your raise; the boss just may go to bat for you.

ASKING FOR BENEFITS

You can request benefits or privileges if you have a valid business-related reason for doing so. Take care to request only those privileges that are truly business-related. Asking to take a client to the boss's ski lodge in Aspen when, in fact, the boss always controls who is invited there is just plain gutsy and may hurt you. On the other hand, if the lodge is clearly meant to be used as company property, and you want to take a very important client there, the risk of asking might pay off. One executive said he would admire any employee who had the nerve to make such a request. Requesting something such as a club membership or an increase in life insurance coverage is more acceptable; the awarding of privileges, either in lieu of or in addition to salary, is anticipated by the top brass. In fact, those who ask are usually the only ones who get.

REFUSING PRIVILEGES, RESPONSIBILITY, AND RAISES

Once in a while it will be to your benefit to assert yourself and decline a promotion or raise that you deem unsatisfactory. This happened a few years ago at a major airline to a woman who had paid her dues for many years and was finally, upon the resignation of her boss, asked to assume responsibility for his job—at considerably less money than he had been making. Rather than throwing a tantrum or lecturing the vice president who offered her the new job—who was himself totally out of touch with what women wanted in business—she simply said that while she was flattered and would like the job very much, it simply was not worth it to her to take on the extra responsibility for so little extra money. She flatly but graciously declined the offer, whereupon the vice president made a trip to personnel to see what they could make of this strange refusal. Fortunately the vice president of personnel was more in tune with the times and suggested that his colleague run back and offer the woman $2000 more than her predecessor had been making. The matter was settled to the woman's satisfaction and no one's ego was wounded.

A similar strategy can be applied to promotions and perks that are not exactly what you wanted.

On the other hand, an executive has to be careful not to assume more responsibility than he or she can handle. Some bosses even try to keep their employees a little overburdened, knowing that a person will have difficulty asking for a raise when he or she is barely getting through each day. Young executives frequently think the most direct route to success lies in being the person who is willing to do anything and everything. Older and wiser executives are rarely caught taking on more than they think they can handle. If your boss pushes you to do too much, use the opportunity to ask for more help, thus expanding your power base. If this is not feasible, request a meeting at which you explain that you fear your work will suffer if you take on too much and that you are at your limit. In one form or another you will most likely be given some help.

A FINAL WORD

Too many people are afraid to ask for what they want, especially in a work situation. Often men are as guilty of this as are women, who can at least offer the excuse that they are fairly new at playing power games. Almost everyone interviewed for this book expressed fear of one or another boss. With age and experience most successful executives overcome this. Oliver Spencer probably summed up this universal fear by saying: "When you start working, you tend to think your boss is brighter, more special, and that's why he is where he is. You respect him just because he is your boss. It didn't occur to me until I was in my thirties that my boss got where he was because two guys ahead of him died, and there wasn't anyone else to replace them with. That's when I lost my reverence for my boss and started asking—and getting—things I wanted and had earned. Today, young executives lose this reverence really young. That's probably good."

CHAPTER 4

The Etiquette
of Communications

B USINESS COMMUNICATION is mostly a matter of common courtesy and involves thinking about how your
method and manner of communication will affect others. For
example, do you frequently use a tape recorder in a meeting when
you could profit more from paying close attention to whoever is
speaking? Do you call in to your office several times if you are
away on business for a few hours? Do you send routine memos to
others without bothering to see whether or not they are read or
desired? Worse still, do you pass along material that comes to you
merely because you are reluctant to throw it away yourself? Do
you make unnecessary copies of letters or other printed materials?
Do you frequently give a secretary a letter to type in final form
only to find you want to make additional corrections when he or
she brings it to you?

If you answered yes to any of these questions, there is a good
chance that you need to brush up on communications etiquette.

Although the purpose of a book on business etiquette is not to
provide a listing of the rules of grammar, it is worth it for you to
consider the more common grammatical errors.

One executive reported in anger: "I recently spent half an hour trying to decipher a totally indecipherable memo. Even the title didn't tell me what the writer was talking about. And then, at the end, there weren't even any suggestions for improving the situation. It was just a meandering piece of writing on someone's equally meandering thoughts on improving some damned minor function of sales. It was, to be honest with you, just an attention-getting device. Well, it certainly got my attention, but not the way the writer hoped, I'm sure."

WRITING BUSINESS LETTERS

Until recently, business letters were written in a stuffy jargon that was a language unto itself. Today, fortunately, the trend is toward more personal expression, and most of the formal, stuffy idioms are no longer used. There is still an art, as well as an etiquette, to writing an excellent business letter. In fact, using the traditional guidelines and format provides an excellent framework for showing communication skills and also demonstrates consideration toward others.

Although a secretary will undoubtedly bear much of the responsibility for the actual preparation of a letter, never forget that your signature goes on it and that the message it carries is a reflection of your business skills. Without looking over someone's shoulder, any executive should routinely read some of the finished letters and all the memos and reports that emerge from his or her office.

There is a right and a wrong way to set up a business letter. This is the right way:

HEADING

342 High Street
Knaw Bone, Indiana 00000
February 28, 1978

Mr. John Walsh
Vice President, Sales
Tobacco Wholesalers Association
3267 North Street
Lexington, Kentucky 00000

INSIDE
ADDRESS

Dear Mr. Walsh:

GREETING

I was delighted to receive your letter last week informing me of the new insurance plan being set up for the growers. It is something tobacco growers have sought for years, and I shall be pleased to be one of the first to join.

BODY

Please do call on me, as you suggested, with additional details. My secretary, Ms. Irma Smithfield, will be pleased to make an appointment for you, and I shall look forward to seeing you again.

Sincerely,

CLOSING

Jack Randolph
President, Randolph Farms, Inc.

SIGNATURE

A business letter, as you can readily note, has six distinct parts: heading, inside address, greeting, body, closing, and signature.

HEADING

In business, and even for personal business correspondence, you will most likely have printed stationery, so the heading often consists of only the date, which is in itself an important detail that should never be omitted.

GREETING

Acceptable greetings for business letters include:

Dear Jack:
Gentlemen: (*or* Ladies: *or* Gentlemen and Ladies:)
Dear Sir or Madam:
Dear Ms. Hindsmith:
   (*or* Miss *or* Mrs.)
Dear Mr. Jackson:

The greeting "My Dear Mr. Trent," once considered more intimate than "Dear Mr. Trent," is not used much today and has become the more formal of the two greetings. Whenever possible, use the name and complete title of the person to whom you are writing.

"Mr.," Mrs.," and "Dr." have long been the only abbreviations used in greetings, but in the past few years, "Ms." has gained popularity, because it serves to take away the distinctions between married and unmarried women. It has become common as a greeting and is perfectly acceptable in a letter today—and even desirable on occasions when you do not know whether you are addressing a single or married woman.

BODY

The body of the letter is where the business is conducted. Most business letters today are quite brief; they rarely run longer than one page, and many run only one paragraph. When a business letter becomes long and complicated, then it is time to consider picking up the phone and calling someone.

Another reason for the brevity of business letters today is that they are often used only to transmit a report, memo, or some other enclosed piece of information. Years ago, such materials were rewritten in letter form; today, memos and reports are often simply forwarded to someone outside the company with a short transmittal note.

Some persons have also adopted the practice of writing a return response on the bottom of a letter they have received, especially when only a line or two is required. This is not a particularly gracious practice, as it seems to be saying to the other person, "Although you showed me the courtesy of a letter, I am too busy to reply in the same manner." There is one time when such a reply might be acceptable, and that is when the sender of the initial letter has indicated that it would be fine for you to reply on the bottom of the page. Even then, the truly gracious gesture is to respond with a short letter on your own letterhead.

In these fast-paced times, it is gracious to resist a telegraphic style when writing business letters. Be sure every sentence is complete and logical, and avoid dropping necessary articles and pronouns.

For example, the following response unintentionally borders on rudeness:

"Received letter December 8. Will advise no later than one week."

Consider how much more gracious is the following:

"I received your letter last week. I do need a couple of days to consider your proposal, but I'll be getting back to you no later than next week."

Whenever possible, in a business letter, use the first person, which is friendlier and more polite. If you are truly using a corporate "we," that is one thing, but when you are the one responding, use "I" whenever possible.

Simple effective language highlights most business letters today. For example:

Avoid these words	*And use these words*
I beg to enclose	I enclose
Please find enclosed	I enclose
Will send same	I shall send you
Yours of the second	Your letter of July 2
Hoping to hear from you	I hope to hear from you
Thanking you	Thank you again *or* I want to thank you again

Avoid these words entirely
And oblige
Beg to advise
In reply I would say

It is appropriate and well-mannered to include some personal greeting or closing in a business letter such as, "Hope you have a very nice weekend" or "I want to wish you and your family a very happy Fourth of July." This is not the same as getting chatty in a business letter, which is an unprofessional thing to do—business letters should be kept as brief as possible—but since the trend is toward conveying the message as quickly as possible, all the more reason to sign off with a cordial line or two.

CLOSING

About the most formal closing ever used today is "Very truly yours," or "Very sincerely." More often, a closing is less formal: "Cordially," "Sincerely," and "Best regards" are frequently used, particularly among persons who regularly write each other.

SIGNATURE

The signature consists of the full name and title of the sender, although it is acceptable to sign only your first name when writing to someone who knows you well. The name and title are always typed, and the signature is always handwritten.

Using Correct Forms of Address

You may have occasion to write to persons of official importance, and there is an etiquette to using their titles both in writing and in speaking. The list that follows shows how to address dignitaries when writing to them and when meeting them.

Titles and Forms of Address

THE PRESIDENT

Address: The President
The White House
Washington, D.C. 20500

Letter opening: Dear Mr. President:
or
Mr. President:

Closing: Respectfully,

Speak of him as: the President

Call him: Mr. President
or Sir

Introduce people to him as: "Mr. President, may I present..."

Say: "How do you do, Mr. President."

THE PRESIDENT'S WIFE

Address: Mrs. John Adams
The White House
Washington, D.C. 20500

Letter opening: Dear Mrs. Adams:

Closing: Sincerely,

Speak of her as: Mrs. Adams

Call her: Mrs. Adams

Introduce people to her as: "Mrs. Adams, may I present..."

Say: "How do you do, Mrs. Adams."

To address them both: The President and Mrs. Adams

UNITED STATES AND STATE SENATORS

Address: The Honorable
James A Michaels
United States Senate
Washington, D.C. 20510
or
The Honorable
John J. Carlson
State Capitol
Springfield,
Illinois 00000

Letter opening: Dear Senator Michaels:

Closing: Respectfully,

*Speak of
him as:* the Senator *or*
Senator Michaels

Call him: Senator Michaels

*Introduce
people to
him as:* "Senator Michaels,
may I present..."

Say: "How do you do,
Senator Michaels,"
or "How do you do,
Senator."

*To
address
Senator
Michaels
and his
wife:* The Honorable
James A. Michaels
and Mrs. Michaels

**MEMBERS OF CONGRESS
OR
STATE LEGISLATURE**

Address: The Honorable
Elizabeth A. Scott
House of
Representatives
Washington, D.C. 20515
or
The Honorable
John A. O'Reilly
State Capitol
Des Moines, Iowa 50300

*Letter
opening:* Ms. Scott:

Closing: Respectfully,

*Speak of
her as:* Ms. Scott

Call her: Ms. Scott

*Introduce
people to
her as:* "Ms. Scott, may I
present..."

Say: "How do you do,
Ms. Scott."

*To
address
Ms. Scott
and her
husband:* The Honorable
Elizabeth A. Scott
and Mr. Scott

**THE CHIEF JUSTICE
OF THE
SUPREME COURT**

Address: The Chief Justice
The Supreme Court
Washington, D.C. 20543

*Letter
opening:* Dear Chief Justice:

Closing: Sincerely yours,

*Speak of
him as:* Mr. Chief Justice
or Mr. Douglas

Call him: Mr. Douglas *or*
Mr. Chief Justice

*Introduce
people to
him as:* "Mr. Chief Justice
may I present..."

or "Mr. Douglas, may I present..."

Say: "How do you do, Justice," *or* "How do you do, Mr. Chief Justice."

To address the Chief Justice and his wife: Chief Justice and Mrs. Douglas

GOVERNORS

Address: The Honorable Carol E. Neely
Governor of California
The Governor's Mansion
Sacramento, California 95800

Letter opening: Dear Governor Neely:

Closing: Respectfully,

Speak of her as: the Governor

Call her: Governor Neely *or* Madam (Sir)

Introduce people to her as: "Governor Neely, may I present..."

Say: "How do you do, Governor Neely."

To address the governor and her husband: The Honorable Carol E. Neely and Mr. Neely

THE MAYOR

Address: The Honorable
David Lindbeck
Mayor of Kewanee
City Hall
Kewanee, Illinois 61443

Letter opening: Dear Mayor Lindbeck:

Closing: Respectfully,

Speak of him as: the Mayor or
Mayor Lindbeck

Call him: Mayor Lindbeck
or Sir

Introduce people to him as: "Mayor Lindbeck, may
I present..."

Say: "How do you do, Mr.
Mayor," *or* "How do
you do, Mayor
Lindbeck."

To address the Mayor and his wife: The Honorable
David Lindbeck
and Mrs. Lindbeck

MINISTER

Address: The Reverend Samuel
George
or The Reverend
Dr. Samuel George

*Letter
opening:* Dear Mr. George:
or
Dear Dr. George:

Closing: Sincerely,

*Speak of
him as:* Mr. (*or* Dr.) George

Call him: Mr. (*or* Dr.) George

*Introduce
people to
him as:* "Dr. George, may I
present..."

*To
address a
clergyman
and his
wife:* The Reverend
Samuel George
and Mrs. George
or
The Right Reverend
Samuel George and
Mrs. George

PRIEST

Address: The Reverend Daniel
W.Williams (*or* other
initials indicating
his order, if he
belongs to one)
Pastor, St. Peter's
Church
Chicago, Illinois 60657

Letter opening: Dear Father Williams:

Closing: Sincerely,

Speak of him as: Father Williams

Call him: Father Williams

Introduce people to him as: "Father Williams, may I present..."

Say: "How do you do, Father Williams," or "How do you do, Father."

RABBI

Address: Rabbi David Rosenberg

Letter opening: Dear Rabbi Rosenberg:

Closing: Sincerely,

Speak of him as: Rabbi Rosenberg

Call him: Rabbi Rosenberg

Introduce people to him as: "Rabbi Rosenberg, may I present..."

Say: "How do you do, Rabbi Rosenberg," or "How do you do, Rabbi."

Using Business Stationery

When you go to work for a company, you will be supplied with printed stationery with the company name and logo and your name and title. Along with stationery invariably come business cards. In many companies, stationery and business cards are supplied automatically, and you have little to say about their quality. When you do have a hand in their selection, order something conservative. The most impressive business stationery is white or buff-colored, is printed in black or another conservative color, and is generally 8½ by 11 inches in size, with matching envelopes.

Business cards should also be conservative. The most tasteful ones show your name and title and the company's name and are printed in black on white or off-white stock. If you have a choice, select a plain typeface.

When you need to order stationery on a new job, simply ask your secretary or the office manager how to go about placing an order.

Using Personal Business Stationery

It is generally a good idea also to keep your personal letterhead in stock; it should follow the guidelines just discussed. The letterhead should contain your name, home address, city, state, and ZIP Code. No reference should be made to your company affiliation on personal stationery, but appropriate titles, such as attorney-at-law, LL.B., Ph.D., or M.D., may be printed after your name. In some professions, it is common practice to print one or more professional affiliations, but in general, omit any but the barest details on personal business stationery. If you have a professional reputation, it will proceed your letters; you need not advertise it.

Writing Letters of Congratulation and Condolence–The Personal Touch

Occasionally you will want to write a personal business letter—to congratulate someone on a promotion, to congratulate an associate whose child graduates from college, to wish someone a good year, or to extend condolences. These letters, with the possible exception of a condolence note, may be typed. It is more gracious if they deliver only their special message and do not contain any business. Keep them short and personal.

A note to express condolences always seems more personal when it is handwritten, although it may be typed if that is your strong preference. It may be composed on the company letterhead.

Only a few lines expressing your sorrow are necessary, particularly if the person who died was not known to you personally. The following is an example of a condolence note to a business associate:

Dear Ben,

I was saddened and shocked to learn of the sudden death of your father last Tuesday. Please accept my sympathy for you and your family. If there is anything I can do, please feel free to call.

Sincerely,

Joe Perez

A congratulatory note can be equally brief:

Dear Janet:

I was recently delighted to learn of your promotion to division vice president. I know you will be an asset to the company in your new position, and I wish you all the luck in the world with your new responsibilities.

Cordially,

Fred Burns

WRITING MEMOS AND REPORTS—WHEN TO USE THEM

Memos and reports are the other two forms of written communication used in most offices. It is especially important to know when to use each channel of communication. As a rule, talking to someone in person results in the greatest degree of mutual understanding, but it can be time-consuming and, unless notes are taken, a conversation can be distorted over time. Written communication is the next most effective method of communicating with someone. When you need to explain something quickly, calling a meeting or writing a memo are the two most effective ways of doing it, although a memo is more considerate of the other person's time. Often when an immediate response is required, phone calls to the individuals involved are the most effective method.

Writing a memo is perhaps the most challenging form of business communication. It is also the form of communication that is most critically read by others. The memo must be brief, to the point and, in many cases, persuasive.

The golden rule in memo and report writing, as in letter writing, is to present a low-key, friendly image. Especially in a memo, in which the main purpose is to convey information, do not talk down to an audience. Avoid discussing annoying or irritating subjects, and do not lecture. Avoid, for example, such condescending expressions as, "of course," "as you know," and "as I was saying."

Conciseness is the key to effective memo and report writing. Go right to the heart of the matter being discussed, which means starting with a title that says exactly what you are going to talk about.

Organize your thoughts before starting to write. One way to do this is to use an old journalist's tip. Divide the information into the following categories: who, what, when, where, why, and how. Then select the most important category and begin with that, working your way through to lesser categories and omitting any category that is plainly not relevant.

Often the line between a memo and a report is unclear. A memo that was passed around to one's coworkers, for example, might well be dressed up as a report and passed on to the top brass.

In either form of writing, always keep your purpose in mind and make sure it is absolutely clear to those who read the material. Furthermore, if you want something, be sure to ask for it—in plain language. Nothing is more exasperating to a busy executive than to waste twenty minutes reading a report outlining a specific problem in the company and then to find no recommendation for solution of the problem.

Don't write anything unnecessary. If it is at all possible to call someone with a request, make that your first option. Persons who turn out memos on a too-regular basis soon find that their master-pieces are rarely read. A memo or a report is a form of personal ammunition, something to be hoarded and used only at the right moment.

Try to avoid emotional overtones in a memo or report or, for that matter, in any form of business communication. Words such as "threat," "hate," "love," "punish"—even the word "should"—used in place of words that suggest rather than demand action sometimes read like rude demands.

It is especially polite when preparing a memo or report to give credit to coworkers when possible.

Before releasing a memo, a report, or even a letter, make it a practice to read it carefully in its final form. You are, after all, the person whose ideas it represents, who knows best what you wanted to say, and who will ultimately be responsible for its contents.

IMPROVING YOUR STYLE

Any form of written business communication should contain the best English you know how to write. The proper choice of words, grammar, and sentence structure are all vitally important in written materials, and errors or carelessness are permanently there for all to see. Substandard English—even a simple word that was accidentally mistyped—may cause the reader to question the writer's ability to communicate and even to think logically.

On the other hand, you should try to avoid writing in a style that is excessively formal or stuffy for this puts the reader off. Long, involved sentences displaying several levels of meaning may have impressed college professors, but they are unimpressive and even damaging in business. While creative writing attempts to convey moods or ideas or to describe characters, almost all business writing is meant to convey facts. There is no place in business writing for convoluted sentences or for words that the reader may have to look up. The object of business writing is to save people, mostly bosses, time. It is rude to write something that attempts to show off what you perceive as your writing skills, with no consideration for the audience to whom the material is directed. Allen Weiss, author of a series of articles on business writing, succinctly summed up what not to do: "For the business writer, self-expression is secondary; self-indulgence is embarrassing, and self-amusement is merely a waste of time."[1] Finally, in writing, as in other areas of getting along with people, avoid negativism. Even when writing about something unpleasant, use positive expres-

[1]Allen Weiss, "The Audience Comes First," *Supervisory Management* 22:2 – 11, (April, 1977).

sions to convey the meaning.

Writing can sometimes be too transparent in exposing a writer's feelings, so carefully check what you have written to be sure it does not show off areas of insecurity or defensiveness.

The most important thing to remember in using written communication is to be considerate of others' time and talent. Always take the audience into account when writing business material and you will be on the road to success.

REVIEWING TELEPHONE MANNERS

The way in which you answer a phone is often enough to determine whether the conversation will go well or badly. If you answer abruptly, you convey the image of an unfriendly, slightly rude person. While it is professional to sound businesslike on the telephone, remember that what you are saying may indeed be held against you if it is not said in a courteous way.

Clarity on the phone is especially important, but rather than asking someone if he or she understands something, adopt such devices as repeating a figure, a statistic, or a key sentence or spelling a name just to be sure that both parties have gotten the facts straight. Also helpful is the practice of keeping a notebook or dictaphone handy to record what you thought a conversation was all about, particularly if there may be ramifications later. Sending a letter of confirmation after an important business call is another way to be sure the matter was understood by all concerned and is a courtesy to the receiver.

How you sound on a telephone is very important. Speak softly out of consideration for others around you, but also speak clearly and slowly so you are understood by the listener.

A cold, expressionless voice does more damage on a phone than it does in person, where your body can show animation even if your voice is less pleasant than it might be, so learn to show interest and liveliness over the telephone.

Answering the Phone

If your calls are screened, you can simply answer by saying, "Hello." If a secretary does not intercept your calls, say something to identify yourself and the company. For example: "Nelson Wade speaking," or "Accounting department, Susy Jones speaking." If the caller asks for someone in the department or for someone you don't know, try to be helpful. Don't say, "Who's this?" or worse still, "You've got the wrong department," followed by a click of the receiver as you hang up. Make an effort to locate the person even if it means giving up a few minutes of your time.

If you are, for some reason, screening a call, ask, "May I say who is calling?" or "May I tell Mr. Smith who is calling?" And remember that the caller has the right to respond, "No, thank you."

If your calls are not screened, answer this way: "This is Frank Ellis." Avoid saying: "This is he," "This is Mrs. Dean," or "Speaking." The latter is merely rude, and the former answers avoid giving your full name, which may be exactly what the caller is hoping to hear.

Making a Call

If a secretary places your calls, as is customary in many companies today, do not waste anyone's time by having the call placed and then keeping the person you called on the line waiting for you to pick up the phone. This is rude and tactless and invariably a sign of a very big ego.

As a matter of fact, many companies interviewed reported that they encouraged executives to place their own phone calls, because this saves time and is more considerate of others—especially secretaries. But if you must ask someone to place a call for you, be right there to pick up the phone when the person you are calling is on the line.

If you reach a switchboard operator when placing a call, say, "Is

Mr. MacAllister there, please?" or simply, "Mr. MacAllister, please."

Identify yourself immediately to the person who next answers, saying: "This is Allen Burke of ABC Company. May I speak to Mark MacAllister, please?"

If you are a frequent caller, say: "This is Al Burke. May I speak to Bill Jones, please?" If you have met the secretary or assistant who answers the phone, a line of greeting to him or her is especially considerate.

Don't say to the person who answers: "Hello, Mr. Dean, please," "Let me talk to Dean," "Dean there?" or "Is Mr. Dean in?" The person who answers the phone should not have to ask who is calling.

If you think the person you are calling may not remember you or recognize your name immediately, repeat it again when he or she comes on the phone, saying: "Hello, Mr. Jones, this is Allen Burke of ABC Corporation. I met you last week during lunch with Bill Jacobson."

If you are calling someone in a specific position, but you do not know the person's name, it is permissible to ask the operator or the person who answers the phone. Say something like this: "Hello. My name is Allen Burke and I am with the ABC Corporation. I am trying to get in touch with your sales manager and wondered if you would be kind enough to give me his name and then ring his phone for me?"

If you reach a wrong number when calling someone, do not hang up but instead say, "Is this 348-6192?" The party who answered will say, "No, it isn't," and you can then apologize and hang up quietly.

If you are connected directly to the person you are calling (one perk for a top executive is a private phone line) or the person answers the phone because a secretary or assistant is absent, do not say: "Is this Mr. Burke?" or "Mr. Burke?" even if you recognize the voice. Instead say, "This is John Smith; is Allen Burke there?" If Allen Burke is polite and sensible, he will not attempt to deny the obvious.

Do not talk to anyone else while you are speaking on the phone, and do not do other work at the same time. If you are unavoidably interrupted, say, "Excuse me a minute, please. I have to handle something." Then cover the mouthpiece and quickly handle the problem. Apologize briefly when you resume the conversation.

Apply the same rules on the phone that you would during any conversation. Listen attentively and do not interrupt, although you may toss in phrases indicating agreement or disagreement just as is done in personal conversation, especially since silences are difficult to interpret over the phone. If you must interrupt someone on the phone, do so graciously.

On the other hand, there is no need to be a captive audience. In a social situation you are expected to wait until the caller signs off. Your business hours, however, are too important to always permit this formality, so if your time is being wasted, sign off gracefully, even if you did not initiate the call. If you are interrupted or are too busy to talk, say so and ask if you may call back, indicating approximately when you will return the call. A particularly gracious way to get rid of a long-winded talker is to say: "I really don't want to take any more of your time, so I'll say goodbye now."

End phone calls by saying "Goodbye." Do not say "Bye-bye" or even "Goodbye now." A goodbye may not even be necessary if it is clear to both parties that the phone call is over.

Directing an Assistant or Secretary to Handle Your Calls

Since your assistant or secretary represents you, it is important to make sure that this person handles your calls the way you want them handled.

Instruct someone taking your calls about whether or not you want to know who is calling before you answer the phone. If you do, tell the person how this information is best obtained, namely, by asking, "May I say who is calling, please?"

If possible, do not ask the person who takes your calls to lie for you. If you cannot come to the phone, your assistant or secretary can say that you are in conference or unavailable, rather than saying you are out of the office when you aren't.

Finally, tell your secretary or assistant politely what you expect a message to contain: accurately spelled first and last names, company name, nature of business, and phone number where you can return the call.

IMPROVING COMMUNICATION SKILLS

Telephone manners are fairly easy to cultivate; writing skills may prove more troublesome, but in either case, the ability to communicate is an important—perhaps *the* most important—skill a manager needs. If you sense that you have problems in this area, look for help. Weak written communication skills can be improved with a good self-help book or textbook. In addition, any serious communicator should have on hand several good style books that will guide him or her in preparing written materials. Among such reference books, the most concise and elegant is *The Elements of Style* by William Strunk and E. B. White. This small volume should be required reading for anyone who ever has to put pen to paper. Another helpful book is *The Careful Writer: A Modern Guide to English Usage* by Theodore M. Bernstein. Because punctuation seems to be a weak area for many business writers, a good book to own is *Punctuate It Right!* by Harry Shaw. All these books assume a degree of literacy and sophistication on the part of their readers; they are in no way guides to better secretarial skills or textbooks on grammar but rather are intended for use by persons who have already acquired the basic skills of communication and who need only to add the polishing touches. Other books on specialized areas of business writing are available in a library or bookstore. One such book is *The Business Writer's Handbook*, by C. Brusaw, G. Alred, and W. Oliu.

CHAPTER 5

Talking Your Way
to the Top

U NLESS YOU ARE REMARKABLY ELOQUENT, and few of us
are, how you speak will not be cause for comment. But if you
speak poorly or massacre your native language, this will indeed be
noticed—and it could be a serious enough offense to stop your
career in midstream.

Poor grammar, like bad breath, is not something your boss will
call you in to talk about improving. Young executives are frequently given guidance on how to manage a project or write a
report, but even your closest friend will not suggest that you leave
something to be desired because of the way you speak. Speaking
poorly may grate on the ears of others, but well-mannered persons
won't tell you about it.

On one level, speaking is idiosyncratic; it is a reflection of
learned patterns of talking and personality. On a deeper and more
important level, it is indicative of the ability to communicate, and
communication is what much of business is all about. A boss who
is able to tolerate too much slang for his or her personal taste will
find it difficult to overlook the kind of speaking that reflects a
confused, illogical mind. Some persons even go so far as to as-

sume, erroneously, that someone who does not have educated speaking patterns is not bright.

Your posture, gestures, and facial expressions can be put to work for you in a powerful way, for body language is just as important as what comes out of your mouth. For proof, turn on your television and watch without the sound; you will be surprised at how well another person's feelings can be detected through gesture and posture. These same signals work when you are with others. They tell your peers that you lack confidence; they tell a boss that you will always be comfortable as his or her subordinate; they say that you want your boss's job. Body language shows when you are pleased, dissatisfied, guarded.

By now you have surmised that speech is not merely what comes out of your mouth when you open it. It is, rather, a subtle interaction of body language and facial expressions, what you actually say, and, perhaps surprisingly, how you listen.

BUILDING SPEAKING SKILLS

The first rule of speaking is: if you don't do it well, do something to remedy the situation. There are numerous books and self-help courses designed to help improve speech. If you suspect that you have a truly bad problem (and get a friend to tell you honestly), take private or group speech lessons, or take acting lessons—but do something.

A good way to know when you have a speech or communication problem is to watch others react to you. Your speech flaws frequently show up in others' responses to you. A long-winded person soon makes everyone in the room uncomfortable; such persons are frequently interrupted; rarely are they listened to with much attention. If you talk too fast or too slow or in an accent that is hard to understand, others will give clues, either by asking you to repeat something several times or by admitting at a later point that they missed "that part of what you said."

Poor grammar or misuse of a word is more difficult to detect since polite persons are trained not to show any reaction to such errors. Try to listen to the speech of others to see how yours differs. At any rate, analyze the effect you have on others, and if you find yourself getting negative signals, take them as a warning that a little self-improvement is in order.

LISTENING

There is an art and an etiquette to being a good listener. Listening is a supreme compliment to others that never fails to reap benefits for the listener. More than one person has been considered a brilliant speaker who was actually a brilliant listener. Listening well means listening raptly. Direct all attention to the person who is speaking. Do not interrupt. Look the speaker directly in the eye most of the time; lean slightly forward and, if possible, sit close to the speaker. Good listeners often have some device—albeit a subconscious one—that shows when their attention has been caught unequivocally. It may be taking off a pair of glasses when the conversation takes a particularly fascinating turn, moving one arm closer to the speaker, or cupping a hand over one ear (usually, this is more likely to be a sign of slight deafness on the part of the listener, but it is, nonetheless, flattering).

Above all, when you are listening to someone else, do not look as if you are mentally planning what you want to say next. Obviously, if you are in an important business meeting or listening to someone speak to an audience, you may have to take a note or two, but in small conversational groups or in one-to-one situations, it is rude to the speaker to appear to be on the verge of breaking into the conversation with your own thoughts.

As a listener, you are expected to react to what you are hearing. This is done largely through body language and a few code sentences or words that have almost symbolic meaning. Such signals stop a speaker from going on about a subject in which the listener has no interest or with which he or she does not agree; they reinforce a speaker one agrees with. As someone talks, be prepared to give signals indicating a reaction to the conversation. Nod yes or no frequently. Slip in such statements as, "I agree completely," "You are absolutely right on that point," or "I can see our thinking is alike on that subject." If you disagree with the point being made, you might say, "We'll have to talk more about that later," "I'll have to give that some more thought," or even simply, "I'm not sure I agree with you on that point." Perhaps the subtlest statement ever heard along these lines is, "You may be right." Spoken in just the right tone, this statement carries the silent implication, "But I doubt it."

Be careful that your body language projects what you are actually thinking as you listen to someone or you will have a misunderstanding to clear up later on in the conversation. For example, do not nod agreement when you do not, merely as a means of encouraging the speaker to go on. At worst, the person may leave the room thinking you agree when nothing could be further from the truth.

USING FLATTERY WISELY

There is an art to flattering someone, and in business, when compliments are often directly related to work, it is particularly important to make flattery work for you.

Flattery has several definitions,[1] two of which are of use in this discussion:

1. To compliment excessively and often insincerely; especially in order to win the favor of; to court; blandish.

2. To portray favorably. To show off.

When going about the business of flattering someone, make very sure that the latter definition is your motive; otherwise the attempt may work to your detriment. False flattery rarely sounds like anything but what is is unless you are complimenting an

---

[1]The American Heritage Dictionary of the English Language (New York: Dell Publishing Co., 1970).

excessively egotistic person who is enormously unsure of himself or herself. And even such a person, when the chips are down, can probably recognize a false compliment.

Two levels of compliments are generally heard in business circles. Level 1 we shall call simple flattery. You like a tie someone is wearing, and you tell him so simply and briefly. A colleague is carrying an especially handsome leather purse; again, you tell her so pleasantly and briefly. These little ego boosts make others feel good, and you need only be careful not to overdo the amount or length of the compliments in this category, lest your power to impress wear thin.

Level 2 compliments, which we shall call serious flattery, should still be honest but can have a definite motive. If, for example, you thought a colleague made an especially good point at a meeting, a well-thought-out compliment can work in your favor in two ways: it flatters the other person and, equally important, it shows you off.

Serious flattery takes a bit more forethought than does simple flattery. It is not acceptable to say (or, worse, to gush): "That speech you gave Tuesday was really dynamite. Just marvelous! How do you do it!" Instead, with a little thought, something like this might better emerge: "I've been giving a lot of thought to the comments you made about reorganizing the order department. Your point about reviewing everyone's workload was especially impressive. I would really like to talk more about it with you some time." With this compliment, you have shown that you truly listened to and thought about the other person's comments; you have made some very specific and honest flattering comments about what he or she said, and you have shown an ability to analyze what others say. If the person you are complimenting is a superior with whom you would not normally initiate a meeting, just omit the last statement of this compliment. The person complimented is sure to remember what you have said and invariably will think more highly of you in the process.

AVOIDING JARGON, CLICHÉS, AND SLANG

Somewhat sadly for the state of the language these days, business jargon has become as common (and offensive to the ears) as the too-frequent use of clichés. Still, its use may be necessary at work. Try not to overuse the jargon that exists where you work; many older executives complain about the lack of good communications skills in young men and women, and your use of jargon could easily be taken as a way of avoiding clear thinking. Besides, being the nonjargon-using speaker on a staff of jargon-loving junior executives could be the factor that sets you apart from the crowd. Examples of business jargon that have crept into the language today and are still best avoided include:

> *utilize* for *use*
> *dialoguing* for *talking* or *conversing*
> *directive* for *memo* or *report*
> *impact on* for *affect*
> *media opportunity* for *press conference*

The list could go on endlessly; the problem is what to do with such expressions. For example, if the term "memo" in your company has been entirely replaced by the word "directive," it is probably more graceful to yield to its use. Perhaps the most useful advice that can be given on the subject is to try to keep the truly insidious expressions out of your speech and writing and to yield to jargon only when *not* using it would label you as a "square" or a "rebel."

The same rules apply for clichés and slang as for business jargon. It's impossible to eliminate clichés and slang from your vocabulary, but use them sparingly, for they may work to convince a superior that you are not an original thinker.

Slang is mostly a way of talking with a peer group. Your boss and other superiors are rarely members of your peer group. They are undoubtedly older, and casual talk among young executives may make them feel older still. Furthermore, the purpose of slang is to display a sense of belonging, to define who is out and who is in—and it just does not make sense to do anything to put one's superiors in such a position. Taken to extremes, this is rude behavior.

You should also be careful to avoid clichés in the decor of your office. A creative, up-and-coming young executive should not decorate his or her office with any form of clichéd expression. This includes cute little figurines with sayings attached, framed sayings, and anything else of this nature. If you want to show signs of personality in your office, do it with an interesting plant or painting.

EXERCISING YOUR WORKING HUMOR

Humor in conversation can be deadly at work if you do not understand its place. The greater success you achieve, the more serious work becomes. Unless you are the president of a company or a chairperson of the board, in which case everyone has to laugh at your jokes, it is not appropriate to open a presentation at a business meeting with an anecdote or joke. In the same vein, don't wisecrack during a meeting or when you are with your superiors, unless you know them very well and can predict that your comments will be well received. Once your bosses have formed an impression of you as the office joker, it will be almost impossible to get rid of it, and you may be overlooked for the important, serious assignments.

TALKING TO AN AUDIENCE

Talking to a group, whether as a postdinner speaker or a television talk show guest, frightens many persons, perhaps because few of us do it on a regular enough basis to truly master the technique. Nevertheless, there will be times when you will be asked to represent yourself and possibly your firm in these ways.

The key to successful public speaking is to prepare yourself and your materials well. As for preparing yourself, attend a speech class or consult a specialist who will teach you how to speak well in public. Buy a good book on the subject; there are numerous ones that help speakers learn how to show themselves off.

Equally important is to prepare what you plan to say. Sometimes your topic is obvious—you are asked to be a guest on a talk show because of something you have written or invented, for example. At other times, such as when you are asked to be a guest speaker at a dinner or lecture, your topic may not be so obvious. In that case, ask. Find out what your topic should be and also what topics anyone else may be speaking on so you do not overlap with other speakers and run the risk of boring your audience.

Research the topic thoroughly, but keep in mind the fact that you are giving a talk, not a term paper or a lecture. However serious your subject, there should be some entertaining moments. On the other hand, too many speakers—even practiced ones—feel the need to open with the obligatory, and usually corny, joke. Add humor only where it is appropriate, and make sure it is sincere and not dated. The best anecdotal materials come from news magazines and newspapers rather than toastmaster's books listing 1,000 of everyone's favorite jokes.

Once you have prepared your material, practice it—over and over and over again. It is better to be so familiar with materials that you cannot go wrong with them than to memorize a speech and run the risk of having a mental block at the last minute.

When the day of the big event arrives, half the battle is won if you have prepared your material and practiced it thoroughly. Do everything possible to make yourself comfortable before you speak. Start by arriving on time. If you are a speaker at a dinner, eat lightly and be careful not to drink too much.

This is one occasion when you will want to be appropriately dressed. Call the chairperson or the person who asked you to speak to find out the appropriate dress. It is also a good idea to find out what color the backdrop is, so you can avoid wearing a color that will clash. Although there are times when you may not mind wearing a dark suit when the dress is black tie, the night when you stand up to speak almost certainly will not be one of them, so plan to dress accordingly.

Once you become comfortable speaking before a crowd, a radio appearance should not pose much of a problem. Television makes many people nervous, but there are a few simple guidelines to help.

Both television and radio are far more intimate mediums than the speaker's dais. When speaking to an audience, while a degree of informality is helpful, you have no reason to seek intimacy. Yet intimacy with the audience is exactly what is required on television. This can be achieved through a balance of talking to the camera (the one with the red light on is the one focused on you) and talking with the talk show host or other persons on the show. Really talk to them, as if you were having an intimate tête-à-tête. Balancing your attention between these two makes the audience feel like part of the presentation and creates a mood of intimacy.

Wear a pastel shirt of any color other than yellow, which photographs as white and is too stark. If you can possibly go without glasses, do so, since their glare is often unflattering. (If you appear on television a lot, it might be worthwhile to purchase a pair of glasses specially treated for television wear.)

Every habit you have will be magnified on television, so be careful not to slump in your chair, jiggle one foot, or exhibit whatever your personal idiosyncrasy happens to be. If at all possible, ask to check your appearance in a monitor before the show begins; this way you will see if you are wearing too much makeup or if your hair is out of place.

MODULATING YOUR VOICE

Modulation refers to the rhythm and tonal quality of your voice. It is especially important not to talk too loudly. No one wants to be caught in the middle of what was meant to be an intimate business lunch with a voice so loud that the entire restaurant knows your company is about to be bought out by a conglomerate.

On the other hand, a voice that is too soft can hurt in a business situation, the most obvious disadvantage being that what you are saying—we shall assume it is something important—simply cannot be heard. Worse still for one's image, a soft voice can make one appear weak and ineffective.

Both men and women who want to be respected and listened to should make an effort to maintain a well-modulated voice most of the time. The modifier "most of the time" is important, because there are times when a lowered or raised voice can be used to make a point especially effectively. This only works, however, when one normally speaks in a well-modulated voice.

Make sure that your voice is pleasant, loud enough to be understood but not so loud that it booms—most of the time.

IMPROVING DICTION

Although diction may be a word you have not heard since grammar school, it refers to the choice of words one makes. Using the wrong word at the wrong time or, for that matter, at the right time, can hurt or even be downright hilarious. A business acquaintance who frequently overextended her vocabulary without first checking definitions once admitted to having had a highly erotic evening when in fact she meant to say she had enjoyed a highly exotic evening. The laugh, unfortunately, was at her expense.

Although there seems to be no reason for many of the distinctions in usage and pronunciation of certain words, knowing how to use words correctly is the mark of an educated person. It is also the mark of a promotable person.

Good English is available to everyone. You may have learned it later than someone whose parents corrected every word, but there is simply no reason not to catch up. The following list consists of words that are frequently misused, to the social detriment of the user.

all the farther When this means "I am going," say, "This is as far as I am going," not "This is all the farther I'm going."

allow and *allow me* This means, "Permit me," not "I allowed as how he was right," an expression that should be banished by a well-intentioned speaker.

an invite The word is "invitation," and nothing else will do.

anywheres, somewheres It seems like such a little thing to attach an "s" to these words, and it is part of the everyday dialect in some cities. Still, try to say "anywhere" and "somewhere."

aunt The broad "a" pronunciation is used on the East Coast, and some persons from other areas of the country may feel illiterate not using this pronunciation; however, the short "a," as in "ant," is perfectly acceptable and nothing to apologize for. Say whatever is comfortable for you.

between and among Between refers to an exchange involving two persons; if there are three or more persons, use "among."

between you and I People who are trying hard to sound literate often use this expression; the correct one is "between you and me."

bad, badly Adverbs, which generally take an "ly" ending, are another example of overdoing it in the name of literacy. The correct answer to "How do you feel?" is "I feel bad." "Feel," a copulative verb, is the equivalent of "am" and takes an adjective. On the other hand, someone does "perform badly." Adverbs can cause problems, but you will do well if you remember to avoid such awkward and pompous expressions as "importantly" and "firstly."

can't hardly This is a double negative; say "I can hardly."

chaise longue You may never have a chance to show this one off, but to do so correctly will show that you know your way around. This is the proper term for what many Americans call "chaise lounge." It is a kind of long chair on which one can semirecline. The last word in this French term is pronounced "long." Never shorten this to "chaise," which only means "chair" in French.

Chinamen and other racial epithets A chinaman is someone in the business of selling fine china; it is never a proper reference to someone from China. A literate (and compassionate) person does well to avoid ethnic slurs of any kind. Among other things, it is just good business: even if you think you can identify ethnic gestures or names, it never pays to risk offending someone.

congratulate Do not pronounce this "congradulate." Do not shorten the word in any way unless you are among old high school buddies and talking about old slang expressions.

consensus This means "agreement of opinion," so it's incorrect to add "of opinion" when you use the word.

dais The platform you stand or sit on at a banquet; pronounce it with a long "a" sound: "da-is," not "di-as."

dialogue Help fight fancy English. Why use this when the word "talk" will do just as well?

egoism, egotism An egoist is someone who tends to see things in terms of how they affect him or her; an egotist is someone who cannot stop talking about himself or herself.

either Either an "e" or an "i" pronunciation is fine.

end result A result *is* the end. Use one or the other.

federal, national "Federal" refers to the government of the United States; "national" conveys a sense of the spirit or patriotism that the citizens feel for their homeland.

fine, splendid, excellent Do not say finely, splendidly, or excellently, when talking about how you feel. Also see *bad*.

folks Avoid using this term to describe your family. "Folk" is correctly used to refer to a people, a nation.

fifth Be careful to sound all the letters.

gent This and other cute nicknames or terms such as "dearie," "honey," "tootsie," "hubby," "little woman," and "girls" (when referring to women) should be avoided; they make most literate persons wince, as well they should.

give me, get me, let me Be sure to pronounce these as two separate words, not as "gimme" or "lemme."

guesstimate This word seems to be worming its way into the language. For the time being, use "estimate" or "guess," depending upon which one you mean.

graduate The verb form should be used as follows: "He was graduated from," or "He graduated from," but not, "He graduated."

high class and other similar expressions Try to avoid saying someone is high class, well-to-do, or wealthy. They are rich. Even if they are not rich, they may be of high quality, but not of high class. Such expressions suggest that you have a sense of inferiority and lack contact with the rich.

hopefully In most sentences "hopefully" is not correctly used, and you can test this by trying to find the word it modifies. Consider: "Hopefully the sales deficit can be made up in the third quart-r." Now see who is hopeful. The sales deficit? Whenever you have the urge to use "hopefully," bite your tongue and instead say, "I hope," which is correct.

house, home This pair is a lot like "national" and "federal." A house is the building. A home is the spiritual place. The correct answer to the question "Where are you?" is "at home," but you are physically in your house.

itch, scratch An itch is the sensation that calls for the act of scratching.

kudos This always takes a singular verb. There is no such thing as a kudo.

lady, woman These are two words that have taken on new significance in the wake of the feminist movement. They seem to be reversing their meanings, with lady now being used disparagingly: "Look, lady, that's your problem." Women today— particularly women seeking equality with men in the professional sphere—frequently resent being referred to as girls, as well they should, since their colleagues would not be overjoyed to be referred to as boys. "Ladies" seems to offend less, but men and women who want to show respect for their colleagues will try to use the word "women." Also see *person*.

leave, let Do not confuse these two words. You leave a room. When someone is detaining you, you may want them to let you go. Do not say, "Leave me go."

lend, borrow You lend something to a friend or acquaintance. They have borrowed something from you.

like This may be the most abused word of our time. It is not a conjunction, as in, "It is cloudy today like it was last Wednesday." Instead say, "It is cloudy today just as it was last Wednesday." Also, if you are describing examples, do not say, "The products are similar to those of our competitors, like the XYZ Co. and Plank Corporation." Instead, say, "The products are similar to those of our competitors, such as the XYZ Co. and the Plank Corporation."

manufacture Pronounce the "*u*" distinctly and do not slip into "man*a*facture."

myself This has come into common usage as a substitute for the correct form of "me" or "I." Just say "I am fine" rather than "I myself am fine" and "as for me" rather than "As for myself."

neither See *either*. This word always goes with "nor," not "or."

off Never use this in place of "from." "I got it off of (*from*) Jane" is
  illiterate.

pardon me This is a rude expression, indicating that you have been
  offended. Instead say, "Excuse me" or "I beg your pardon."

person Terms such as salesperson and chairperson have gained
  wide usage today, despite their seeming awkwardness. Few
  women object, and many men and women are now using the
  terms with ease. There is really no etiquette on this subject,
  except that each person should do what is comfortable for
  him or her and, more important, for those to whom the terms
  will be applied.

personal friend Just the word "friend" will suffice. Friends are
  always personal.

the reason why, the reason is because "Reason" means "why" and
  "because"; therefore, say, "The reason is that . . ."

restroom, bathroom Restroom is generally used to refer to public
  bathrooms, at work, in hotels, and anywhere outside the
  home; bathroom is used at home.

second Be sure to pronounce the "d."

sore This is how you feel when something hurts. It is not a
  substitute for "angry."

strength Pronounce every letter, taking special care not to omit the
  "g."

tomato See *aunt*, and stick to saying tomato the way you learned to
  in the old neighborhood.

you know This has filtered into the language to an incredible
  degree; and while there is nothing grammatically wrong with
  it, it irritates a lot of persons who were born before it came
  into common usage.

yeah The same thing applies here. You take your chances when
  you use this word in the business world; it is a sign of sloppy
  thinking.

REVIEWING FOREIGN WORDS AND PHRASES

Familiarity with some foreign words and expressions is the mark of an educated person, to say nothing of the fact that it will help you order food in a French restaurant, find the right train in Germany, and read some scholarly works. The most commonly used foreign words and phrases come from French, German, and Latin.

A word of warning here: knowledge of foreign words and expressions should be put to discreet use. Sprinkling one's conversation with foreign words does not show that one is well-travelled; it indicates that one is showing off. A parallel can perhaps be drawn between knowing and using foreign expressions and knowing how to play a bagpipe: a gentleman, it has been said, is someone who knows how to play the instrument but refrains from actually doing so.

The best way to feel secure in using foreign expressions is to hear someone else speak them, so don't be shy about asking an expert speaker in a language how to say something or taking a few language lessons. There are also many good books on foreign grammar and speaking that will help you become familiar with useful expressions.

REVIEWING FOREIGN MENU TERMS

The foreign terms that Americans are most likely to come into contact with are those found on menus in French restaurants. Here is a list of the most commonly used expressions:

agneau	lamb
ail	garlic
à la	in the style of
amandine	made with almonds; often used in preparing fish fillets
ananas	pineapple

anchois	anchovy
anglaise, à la	cooked in either water or stock
artichauts	artichokes
artichauts à la vinaigrette	artichokes in olive oil and garlic
asperges	asparagus
assiette anglaise	assortment of cold cuts
aubergine	eggplant
au jus	in its own juice
au lait	with milk
avocat	avocado
baba au rhum	cake soaked in rum after it has been baked
banane	banana
basilic	basil
béarnaise	thick sauce made with shallots, tarragon, thyme, bay leaf, vinegar, white wine and egg yolks, served with grilled or sautéed meat or grilled fish
béchamel	sauce of milk thickened with butter and flour
beurre d'ail	garlic butter
beurre noir	brown butter served on eggs, fish, or vegetables
bière	beer
biscuits	cookies
bisque	soup, usually made of puréed shellfish
blanquette de veau	veal stewed in a cream sauce
boeuf	beef
boeuf bourguignon	braised beef prepared in the style of Burgundy (with small glazed onions, mushrooms and red wine)
boeuf rôti	roast beef

bombe glacée	ice cream dessert
bon bon	candy
bonne femme, à la	cooked with bacon, onions, potatoes and a thick brown gravy
bordelaise	brown sauce made with wine and bone marrow
boudin	blood sausage
bouillabaise	fish chowder from French Riviera; made with fish, olive oil, tomatoes, and saffron with water or bouillon
bouilli	boiled
braisée	braised
brioche	a kind of French bread
brochette	a skewer; anything cooked on a skewer may be called a *brochette*
brocoli	broccoli
brouillé	scrambled
café glacé	ice cream with coffee flavoring
calmar	squid
canapé	a small round of bread, topped with various spreads and used as an appetizer
canard	duck
canard à l'orange	duck in orange sauce
caneton	duckling
câpres, sauce aux	caper sauce, used most often on lamb
carbonnade à la flamande	beef cooked with beer
carottes	carrots
cassoulet	stew made with white beans and pork
cervelles	brains
champignons	mushrooms
châteaubriand	cut of beef, grilled and served with vegetables cut in strips and with a *béarnaise* sauce

choix	choice
choux de bruxelles	Brussels sprouts
ciboulette	chives
citron	lemon
coeur d'artichauts	artichoke hearts
compote de fruits	stewed, mixed fruit (fresh or dried), served cold
consommé	meat stock that has been enriched, concentrated, and clarified
coq au vin	chicken in a red wine sauce with mushrooms, garlic, small onions, and diced pork
coquillages	shellfish
coquille St. Jacques	scallops
cornichon	type of small pickle, served with pâté and other dishes
côte de boeuf grillé	grilled beef rib
côte de veau	veal chop
courgette	zucchini
crabe	crab
crème	custard or cream
crème brûlée	a rich dessert pudding made with vanilla and cream, which is lightly coated with sugar, placed under the broiler, and then cooled for two to three hours before serving
crème caramel	custard with a burnt sugar flavor
crème Chantilly	whipped cream
crêpes	thin pancakes
crêpes Suzette	thin dessert pancakes topped with a sauce made with curaçao and the juice of mandarin oranges, usually served flaming
crevettes	shrimp

croissant	crescent-shaped roll made with a puff pastry or yeast dough; most often served at breakfast
croque madame	grilled chicken and cheese sandwich
croque monsieur	ham and cheese sandwich, fried
croûtons	bread that has been diced and sautéed in butter; used in soup and on salads
crudités	raw vegetables served as an appetizer
cuisses de grenouilles	frogs' legs
daube	chunks of meat stewed with vegetables
demiglace	a thick, brown sauce
demitasse	strong, black coffee served in a small cup
diable, sauce à la	spicy sauce of white wine, vinegar, shallots, and pepper
dinde	turkey
dolmas	stuffing wrapped in a vine leaf
duglère, à la	with a cream sauce made with wine and tomatoes, served with fish
échalotte	shallot
écrevisse	crawfish
en croûte	baked in a pastry crust
entrecôte	translates as "between the ribs"; steak cut from between two ribs of beef, usually grilled or fried
entrecôte marchand de vin	steak cooked with red wine and shallots
épinards	spinach
escalopes de veau	thin, boneless slices of veal
escalopes de veau cordon bleu	thin slices of boneless veal with ham and cheese

escargots	snails
farci	stuffed
filet de boeuf	tenderloin
filet mignon	small, choice cut of beef prepared by grilling or sautéeing
flambé	describes a dish that has been ignited after being doused in a liqueur
florentine, à la	foods cooked in this style (usually eggs or fish) are put on spinach, covered with mornay sauce, and sprinkled with cheese
foie	liver
foie gras	the livers of fattened geese and ducks
fraises	strawberries
framboises	raspberries
frappé	chilled
frites	french fries
fromage	cheese
fruits de mer	seafood
garni	garnished or decorated
gâteau	cake
gigot d'agneau	leg of lamb
glace	ice cream
gratin, au	prepared with a topping of toasted breadcrumbs; usually includes grated cheese
hareng	herring
haricots	beans
herbe	herb
hollandaise	sauce made with egg yolks and butter; served over vegetables and fish
homard	lobster
hors d'oeuvres	appetizers, hot or cold
huîtres	oysters

jambon fumé	smoked ham
jardinière, à la	fresh vegetables, served with roast, stewed, or braised meat and poultry
julienne	meat or vegetables cut into thin strips
lait	milk
laitue	lettuce
lapin	rabbit
légumes	vegetables
lyonnaise	prepared with onions
macédoine	fruit or vegetables, diced and then mixed
madeleine	sweet made from flour, butter, eggs, and sugar baked in shell-like molds
madère, sauce au	sauce made with Madeira wine
madrilène	clear chicken soup with tomato; served chilled
maison	a term applied only to recipes that are exclusive to the restaurant's owner or chef but usually used more loosely to mean in the style of the restaurant
marchands de vin, sauce	brown sauce of butter and red wine
maître d'hotel	headwaiter
médaillon	food cut into a round or oval shape
menthe	mint
meunière	method of preparing fish; the fish is first seasoned, floured, and fried in butter, then served with lemon juice, parsley, and melted butter
mornay	white sauce wth cheese added
moules	mussels
mousse	a light, airy dish made with cream and eggs; may be of fish, chicken, fruits, or chocolate; served hot or cold

moutarde	mustard
nature	plain; without trim; in its natural state
niçoise, à la	a dish cooked in the style of Nice, often prepared with tomatoes, zucchini, garlic, potatoes, green beans, olives, garlic capers and anchovies
nouilles	noodles
oeuf	egg
oeufs à la Russe	hard-boiled eggs with a mayonnaise sauce of chives, onion, and a dash of tabasco
oeufs bénédictine	in most American restaurants this refers to an egg and ham on an English muffin with hollandaise sauce and possibly a slice of truffle
oignon	onion
omelette	omelet; an egg dish
omelette aux fines herbes	omelet made with parsley, tarragon, and chives or another combination of herbs
pain	bread
palourdes	clams
papillote, en	steamed, enclosed in a sheet of parchment
parfait	an iced dessert
pâté	any dish of ground meat or fish baked in a mold that has been lined with strips of fat
pâté maison	a pâté unique to a particular restaurant
pâtisseries	pastries
pêche	peach
pêches melba	peaches that have been steeped in vanilla-flavored syrup, served over vanilla ice cream topped with raspberry purée
petit-beurre	butter cookie

petite marmite	clear soup made with meat, poultry, marrow bones, stock pot vegetables, and cabbage; usually served with toast and sprinkled with grated cheese
petit pain	roll
pilaf	rice sautéed in oil and cooked with a variety of seasonings
poisson	fish
poivre	pepper
pomme	apple
porc	pork
potage	soup, usually with cream base
pot-au-feu	French version of the boiled beef dinner
pots de crème au chocolat	rich chocolate dessert
poulet	chicken
poulet à la Marengo	a method of cooking chicken by browning it in oil, adding wine, and serving it with a garnish of fried eggs, mushrooms, and crawfish
poulet chasseur	chicken prepared with sautéed mushrooms, shallots, and white wine and tomatoes
poulet rôti a l'estragon	roast chicken with tarragon
printanière, à la	garnished with a variety of spring vegetables
prix fixe	at a set price
profiterole	eclair-like pastry; may be filled with ice cream, any purée, or a custard, jam, or other sweet filling
provençale, à la	cooked in the style of Provence, usually with tomatoes, garlic, olives, and eggplant

purée	food that has been mashed or put through a sieve or processed in a blender
quenelles	dish made with ground fish or meat blended with cream
quiche Lorraine	a tart made with eggs, cream, cheese, and bacon
ragout	a dish made from meat, poultry, or fish that has been cut up and browned; may or may not include vegetables
ratatouille	a mixture of eggplant, zucchini, squash, onions, tomatoes, and peppers; may be served hot or cold
ravigote	a white sauce, hot or cold, highly seasoned with thyme and coarsely ground black pepper
reine de saba	cake of chocolate, rum, and almonds
ris de veau	sweetbreads of veal
riz	rice
Robert	sauce of onion, white wine, and mustard; served with grilled pork dishes
rognons	kidneys
saucisson	large sausage; sliced for serving
saumon	salmon
sec	dry
sel	salt
sorbet	sherbet; made from fruit or liqueurs
soufflé	dish made with puréed ingredients, thickened with egg yolks and beaten egg whites; may be made with vegetables, fish, meat, fruit, nuts, or liqueurs; served as an appetizer, a main dish, or a dessert
specialité de la maison	specialty of a particular restaurant

steak au poivre	steak made with crushed peppercorns
steak tartare	uncooked ground meat seasoned with salt and pepper and served with a raw egg yolk on top and with capers, chopped onion, and parsley on the side
sucre	sugar
suprêmes de volaille	chicken breasts
sur commande	made to your special order
tarte	pie
thé	tea
tournedos	small slice of beef, round and thick, from the heart of the fillet of beef; sautéed or grilled
tranche	slice
truffe	truffle, a fungus that grows underground
truite	trout
varié	assorted
vichyssoise	a cream soup of leeks, potatoes, and chicken broth; served cold
vin	wine
vinaigrette	sauce of oil, mustard, and vinegar, seasoned with salt and pepper and, at times, herbs
volaille	fowl, poultry

PRACTICING—A FINAL WORD

The key to improving your speaking skills is practice. Watch others, and when you see something you like that you think will work for you, adapt it to your speech. If you know you have a serious problem communicating—you are too shy to speak in front of an audience, yet your work demands that you do so several times a year; you know you talk too long whenever you make a presentation, or you simply never had the opportunity to learn correct English—take private speech lessons, acting lessons, or any other speech class that might help you.

It *is* true that speech is a sign of good manners. But it is one of the signs that anyone can acquire without too much effort.

CHAPTER 6

The Business Lunch
and
Other Public Entertainments

T HE WHEELING AND DEALING that goes on over lunch these days has reached mythic proportions. Such lunches—always paid for with "plastic"—often last two or three hours and the tab may run to $100 or more for two, but then multibillion-dollar business mergers, million-dollar book deals, and even million-dollar raids by one corporation of another's top executives are often the goal of such meetings.

Regardless of whether or not you are involved in such high-level lunching, don't underestimate the value of sitting down over a meal to hammer out a business deal—or even merely to build a relationship prior to talking business—and never underestimate how devastating not being able to handle that lunch can be. The business lunch has become so important that, at this writing, one Eastern school teaches a two-semester, three-credit course called "The Dynamics and Management of the Business Lunch"—and it's required for the master's program.

The business lunch—or any other business entertainment, for that matter—is where all your social skills and graces come together: table manners, your abilities as a host or hostess, your ability to speak well, your ability to handle others—all must be in peak working order. In Japan, many centuries ago, a man could be executed for exhibiting poor table manners. While none of the executives we have talked with have gone quite that far, many have noted the lack of finesse often displayed in this all-important area.

Business lunches are for business, and often one or the other party to such a lunch makes it clear that this will be a working lunch. Usually though, the business conducted is minor, or the lunch is merely a prelude to business that will be conducted later. The point is that because any business could be accomplished without the accoutrements of a meal, there is an underlying reason for planning to lunch or even dine with a client or employee. That underlying reason is camaraderie, which in the case of the business lunch is not necessarily a reference to a strong, personal, social relationship but, rather, refers to the kind of relationship that enhances whatever business is involved.

One executive, in describing his long-standing relationship as a consultant to Oscar Meyer, put his finger on the role of business lunches in fostering good work relationships: "For twenty-odd years, I've been a consultant to Oscar Meyer Company. There is no question in my mind that I would not have had that continuing relationship if the executive committee of that company were not very comfortable with me in the executive dining room. I'm so easy to replace; I'm here in Chicago, they're in Madison. I don't have a personal relationship, but I have a very comfortable business relationship. I think if there were *anything* about me that irritated them in the executive dining room, they would have terminated our relationship."

There are two underlying purposes for a business lunch. First, there is the lunch that, on the surface, appears to be purely social. Its purpose is to establish or strengthen the informal business bonds just described or even to woo a client so he or she will lean a little bit more toward your company or product when making a decision.

Second, there is the working lunch, at which the participants have agreed, usually in advance, that business will be discussed. This kind of lunch may even have an agenda, and when an invitation is extended, the host or guest might say, "Fine, then, we'll have lunch Tuesday to discuss those details of the contract that need working out."

Business lunches are also used to evaluate prospective employees, and among employees to celebrate a raise or promotion, to talk over a new position within a company, or by employers to woo an unhappy executive. Some bosses have even used the business lunch to fire, but this has never been recognized as being particularly good for anyone's digestion.

PLANNING THE LUNCH

Setting up a business lunch is relatively easy to do. Invariably it is done by phone. If you are planning the lunch, make it clear that you expect to be the host, possibly by saying, "How about having lunch with me next week?" or "I've been hoping we could get together over lunch to discuss the merger. How does some day next week sound?" Since it is presumed that all parties involved share an interest in getting together, a business lunch invitation is left more open than a purely social invitation with regard to time. Suggesting a lunch "next week" lets the person invited check his or her calendar and come up with an appropriate date. If the date suggested is not open for you, come up with an alternate day. Remember that the purpose is to find a mutually agreeable time and that business lunches among busy persons are often scheduled far in advance.

Once you have settled on the day, another way to make it clear that you will be host is to say, "How about The Four Seasons?" or "How about the Town Club? They have excellent steaks there."

Confirm the time and place and repeat the details of the invitation later in the conversation. At the end of the call, you might say, "Fine, then I'll see you next Tuesday, the fifteenth, at 1 P.M. at the Town Club—let's meet in the downstairs lobby."

Local custom will generally dictate the time of the lunch. In large cities, lunches are often planned at 1 P.M., and a 2 P.M. lunch date is not unheard of; in smaller communities, where persons are less likely to linger even over an important business lunch, 12 P.M. or even 11:45 A.M. may be more common.

The choice of the restaurant is important, although it may be fairly obvious. An important business lunch calls for an elegant restaurant. In a small town or city, there may be only one or two such restaurants; in Chicago, San Francisco, Los Angeles, and New York, certain restaurants are frequently the "in" places for lunch for persons in certain professions.

If possible, pick one restaurant and frequent it; this will pay special rewards in terms of your being recognized when you walk in, and it will probably result in better service. Of course, recognition and service are not necessarily automatic—you will have to cultivate and tip the headwaiter to make yourself known. But for making a subtle impression, little beats having the headwaiter ask if you will have your usual drink or your usual lunch.

In addition, always make reservations. If the restaurant is good, they will be absolutely necessary, and even if it is not busy, as happens in small towns, a call ahead still alerts the staff that you are planning a special lunch.

ARRIVING AT THE LUNCH

Since you are presumably the host, it is polite to arrive before your guests. If you are late, apologize briefly. If the guests arrive later than you do, wait for them in the lobby or wherever you agreed to meet.

When a guest arrives, ask if he or she wants to check his or her coat. When this is done, give the headwaiter your name if you are not known, and let your guests precede you into the dining room.

OFFERING SPECIAL AMENITIES TO FEMALE GUESTS

Chapter 12 covers ways a woman with close feminist feelings can make her views known in a business situation if she feels she must do so. And certainly any man entertaining or even maintaining a business relationship with a woman these days should be aware of the nuances that are possible in male-female relationships. Many very powerful women want—and expect—all the traditional amenities to be paid to them—doors opened, coats taken, chairs pulled out. Younger women executives may be less than eager to receive such attentions, but many are quite willing to go along with the more traditional amenities for the sake of a smooth social relationship. After all, the point of a business lunch is to conduct business, not to work out a personal relationship. Even subversive power struggles between men and women can serve to put a damper on the atmosphere—regardless of who initiates them. So if you are a man entertaining a woman, be prepared to take a clue from her as to how she wants to be treated. And if you are a woman entertaining a man, it is equally tactful to keep his social values in mind.

Men usually open any doors that need opening. If a woman does not move away from you to take off her coat, offer assistance. A tactful and even a militant feminist would be less than gracious to make a point of not letting someone do this once the action has been initiated. In the dining room, a man may or may not—depending upon what he knows about the woman's personal feelings—hold out the chair for her. One custom that has entirely fallen by the way these days at business encounters is for men to order the meal for women. Unless a woman is very Old-School and tells you what she wants to order and then looks at you when the waiter arrives, assume that any woman is quite capable of placing her own drink and food order.

ORGANIZING THE SEATING

As the planner of a business lunch, the host can suggest where the guests may sit. If two persons are lunching at a table for four and you know you will need some space to spread out papers, you may have a very specific reason for wanting the other person to sit to your right or across from you.

Occasionally banquettes pose a slight problem, particularly when a man and woman are lunching for purposes of business. If you are really uncomfortable with a banquette, where you are usually expected to sit alongside the person you are eating with, request a table when you make the reservation.

SMOKING AND NOT SMOKING

If you don't want someone to smoke in your presence because you are a nonsmoker, or if you, a smoker, insist upon your right to smoke, then smoking is a cause for you, and you probably don't want any polite ways to handle the situation. If, however, you want to know the etiquette of smoking (and nonsmoking), here are a few guidelines.

Smoking is frequently annoying to a nonsmoker, and some persons are allergic to smoke. So before you light up, always ask if the other person minds. There are some times not to smoke, and one of these is before everyone at a table has finished eating. If you can control yourself, it is also considerate not to smoke between courses. Then, too, a smoker should keep an eye on the direction the smoke is going. Move an ash tray or cigarette away from another person's face if the smoke is going toward him or her.

If you are a nonsmoker or are allergic to smoke, you must be assertive enough to tell someone you would prefer that they not smoke in your presence. Try not to make an issue of this, however, and when someone asks if you mind their smoking, say that you have a mild allergy and would prefer that they did not.

Many restaurants today are divided into smoking and nonsmoking sections, which does pose a problem if one person smokes and the other one doesn't. There is no easy solution to this problem. If you are entertaining an important client who smokes, and you think you can tolerate the smoke, the gracious thing to do is to offer to sit in the smoking section. On the other hand, any smoker who is not totally addicted should offer to sit in the nonsmoking section. If one person has an allergy or health problem, there is no need to try to reach a compromise: you must sit in the nonsmoking section.

ORDERING DRINKS

As soon as you are seated, the waiter will probably take your drink order. Don't put a guest on the spot with regard to deciding whether or not to order a drink. Drinking has become a totally accepted part of business lunches, and even if someone does not drink, there is no reason to make anyone else at the table feel uncomfortable about this. When the waiter asks whether you would like drinks, look at your guest and say, "Yes, I would, what will you have?" The guest can then order his or her usual drink, and you can order your usual drink—even if it is nonalcoholic.

If you are a nondrinking guest and drinks appear to be the order of the day, order something—sparkling water with lemon or lime, ginger ale, a virgin mary—and make no comment about the fact that it is nonalcoholic. The host should still feel at ease enough to order whatever he or she usually drinks.

What isn't accepted at lunch in most professions and companies is heavy drinking. While the drink before lunch may be a formality that leads to an air of informality, ordering two or three drinks—whether you are the guest or the host—can spell disaster.

For starters, it shows less than serious intentions about the business nature of the lunch and, for another, it may wipe you out so you cannot conduct even lunch seriously. Especially in these days of expensive lunches, few persons are willing to foot the bill for someone who can't handle drinking—and a guest (a potential customer or client) has to think twice about how the host will handle any business if he or she can't handle alcohol over lunch. So unless you are very good friends and know in advance that you and your guest will indulge in a bout of serious lunchtime drinking every so often, limit yourself to one or two drinks.

ORDERING FOOD

There is even an art to what you order to eat these days. While it has always been slightly gauche to eat as if you were going to your execution right after lunch, in these days of physical fitness and diet consciousness, business lunches often become contests between the eaters to see who can eat the least. Dessert is rarely ordered today; sauces are passé at lunch; and salads, fish platters, and cheeses are *de rigueur*. But a word of warning: If you're on a diet, keep quiet about it. Everyone has talked the subject to death, and no one really wants to hear about anyone's diet over lunch.

PLAYING HOST

A host at a business lunch should show the same concern for guests in a restaurant as he or she would at home. Ask the waiter to fill the water glasses, empty the ash trays, or do whatever appears to be needed. If a guest is displeased with the food—it is too hot or too cold or too rare or too well done—be sure it is sent back to the kitchen, unless the guest protests strongly against it.

When the meal (and your business) is finished, ask the waiter for the check. If you are at a favorite haunt, the waiter will have no doubt about bringing the check to you; in an unfamiliar restaurant, the person who asks for the check is the person who gets it.

Sometimes a waiter will automatically bring the check to a man when a woman is present. If you are a woman and the host, simply reach over and take the check—don't grab, but make a firm gesture. If necessary, reassure your lunch guest that "It's all on my company, anyway." You can go to some elaborate lengths to ensure that you do indeed pay the check; pretending to go to the restroom and then paying the maître d'hotel or arranging to pay in advance are two of the more common ploys, but these should hardly be necessary today. Most men, when they have been invited to a business lunch, have no qualms about letting a woman who is representing her company pick up the check. If a man is really Old-School and you sense that he would be ill at ease sitting by while a woman pays, then acquiesce after minimal fuss and let him pay.

A host of either sex should look the bill over quickly and carefully. Figure out the tip and place your credit card (or money, if you must) on the tray, with the check turned face down. Don't leave pennies, nickels, or dimes as part of the tip, except when the waiter brings change near the amount of the tip. Then leave all the change. If you pay a cashier and do not have change for the tip when you leave the table, ask the cashier for change and walk back to the table to put it down. Even if a guest offers to pay all or part of a tip when it is obvious that you don't have the needed change, do not accept. The chart on pages 115-117 shows guidelines for tipping. In expensive restaurants and in places you frequent for business, 15 to 20 percent is the usual tip; 25 percent is showing off, and 10 percent is not enough.

PLAYING GUEST

As the guest at a business lunch or other entertainment, you take no notice of the check, but you do thank your host when you are saying goodbye. If you are invited to lunch at one of the fancier private corporate dining rooms, all you need to do to get through the occasion—aside from displaying your most perfect manners—is to stay cool. Act as if you are used to dining this way, even if your company's corporate dining room looks like the Marines' mess. Do not permit yourself to be impressed—or if you are, do not let it show. Act as if this were the most routine of lunches. Of course, if your host has just spent the last six months of his or her work life redecorating the dining room or interviewing for just the right French chef, there is nothing wrong with showing your appreciation—in your normal, low-key way.

GUIDELINES FOR TIPPING

PERSON	SERVICE	AMOUNT
Maître d'hotel	Checks your reservation and shows you to your table.	No tip
	If he arranges tables to accommodate a large group or seats you without a reservation when one would normally be needed or performs any other special service.	$1 to $3
Captain	Takes drink order, explains dishes on menu, recommends dishes, carves rack of lamb or any special food, flambées a food.	5 percent of total bill, never less than $1
Waiters, waitresses	Serve food.	15 percent of bill

PERSON	SERVICE	AMOUNT
Bartender,	When drinks are served at a bar.	10 to 15 percent, minimum 50 cents
Busboy	Clears dishes, pours water, refills coffee.	No tip (he shares with waiters)
Strolling musicians To get rid of them.		$1
To request a medley or song.		$2 or more
Restroom attendant		50 cents minimum, if any service is provided
Checkroom attendant		50 cents minimum per coat
Doorman	Opening door.	No tip
	Parking car.	50 cents minimum
	Hailing cab.	50 cents minimum
	Hailing cab in bad weather.	50 cents to $1
Taxi drivers		Rarely is less than 25 cents given today for any length of ride. When fare is between 50 cents and $1.25, give 25 to 35 cents. When fare is over that, give 15 percent.
Skycap	Handles bags in airport.	50 cents per bag; more for large bags or trunks

PERSON	SERVICE	AMOUNT
Redcap	Handles bags in train station.	There is usually a set fee of about 50 cents; add a dime or two or more in addition if service is greater.

INTRODUCING BUSINESS DURING LUNCH

Don't be misled by a festive atmosphere at lunch when you have agreed to discuss business. Most executives, however congenial or mellow they may become during lunch, still intend to discuss the subject at hand if that was prearranged—and many top executives whose time is very valuable expect business to be discussed even if no previous mention was made of this fact. Not to discuss business at a business lunch is not necessarily congenial; it is a waste of time and may put off a busy, organized person.

Generally the host initiates the business discussion, and a smart host takes the opportunity to do so before a busy guest gets impatient and beats him or her to the draw. Business, if not urgent, is often discussed more toward the end of the meal or over coffee. Don't wait too long, though, or you won't have time to accomplish your objective. If you have both agreed that this will be a working lunch, the direct approach is the best way to settle down to the work at hand. Simply say, "Well, shall we talk about the new contract?"

If the business to be discussed is more subtle, you would be more likely to ease into the discussion, saying something such as, "Well, what do you think about the proposed merger?" or "While it's on my mind, I've been meaning to ask you about the new product line."

ENDING THE LUNCH

If you are discussing business, the lunch may continue long into the afternoon, although this is rare. As a rule, the person who is hosting the lunch is the first to lay his or her napkin back on the table or to stand, thereby signaling the end of the meal. Asking the waiter for the check is also a signal that the lunch is about to end.

One good rule about ending a business lunch is to assume that the other person has other things to do that afternoon. Even if you are wooing a client to close a very big deal, you may lose his or her respect—and the account—if you act too casual about prolonging a lunch.

ENTERTAINING ON PREMISES

Since major corporations have established corporate headquarters outside major cities, on-premises entertaining has become an increasingly popular way to entertain. It began as a means of feeding employees lunch when they had nowhere else to go, but it has emerged into full-blown, elaborate, and luxurious executive dining rooms, and some companies have even hired specially trained chefs who can prepare elaborate meals for their clients and customers on their own business premises.

While an order-in lunch for a company's executives can be handled by a secretary, the kind of elaborate, carefully planned, on-premises entertaining that many major corporations are now using is coordinated or overseen by the executive who is host. After all, having twenty of your most important customers into your plant to introduce a new product line takes a lot of well-coordinated planning. In return, it offers more control, a chance to show off your offices or plant, and a more casual way of selling your products. One major manufacturer in New Jersey introduces a new line by busing in clients for a champagne and omelette breakfast.

"It simply works better," the sales manager of the company reported. "I know how much time will be spent eating and drinking. I can casually move the clients toward the product displays. Everything is much more soft-sell—the mood is festive. The sales people simply circulate among the customers; there is no reason for them to push."

Acquiring an appreciation of the benefits of on-premises entertaining is easy enough, but many managers are unsure of how to go about setting up this entertainment. First, go over old entertaining budgets in company records to get some idea of what catering fees have been in the past. Call in one or two top caterers and discuss your plans with them. A caterer needs to know the time frame, the desired atmosphere, and exactly what you need to achieve. The days are long gone when caterers planned ladies' lunches and little else. Any professional caterer is geared to business entertainment; all know how to help show off a product line, entertain your top four customers at a formal dinner and, most important, how to control the time and money spent in doing so.

Above all, be open with the caterer about what you can spend. On-premises catering is generally cheaper than other kinds of entertaining anyway, so you may be able to plan a more elegant function than you realize. On-premises entertaining is less sterile and certainly less hard-sell than similar functions in hotels or rented halls.

If you have hired a caterer who comes highly recommended and you do not know much about food and food service, rely on the caterer's advice. A service representative, however, always enjoys working with someone who does have menu suggestions, so don't be afraid to offer ideas if you have them. On the other hand, several caterers interviewed complained that persons who have not had a good deal of experience in planning this kind of entertaining often become too involved. Remember that the caterer's business is providing food and service; just as you delegate other aspects of managing your business domain, be willing to do so with food service when you know you are dealing with professionals. And treat the caterer with courtesy; he or she will only work that much harder for you if made to feel good about doing so.

ENTERTAINING AT PRIVATE CLUBS

If you are a member of a private club, the club is often an ideal place to entertain business associates. Among other advantages, cash is almost never used, so there is never any question about who picks up the tab.

If you are invited to be a guest at a private club, you behave exactly as you would in any public restaurant. If you arrive before your host, you will probably be shown to a waiting room or lounge; wait there until your host arrives. If you want a brief tour of the place, ask your host; don't roam around by yourself.

It is assumed that you are a nonpaying guest at a private club, so do not offer to pay for anything. Even offering to pay for a round of drinks may prove difficult since money is rarely used in private clubs.

Sports at Private Clubs

If you are invited to play golf or tennis at a private club to which you do not belong, you are not expected to pay. You are expected to dress appropriately and, in many cases, conservatively, for the sport. Tennis whites are often the rule, and appropriate footwear is a necessity. You bring your own sports equipment.

ENTERTAINING ON A BOAT OR SHIP

Regardless of the size of the craft (any boat longer than 100 feet is technically a yacht), owners of sailing vessels refer to their crafts as boats and to themselves as sailors. So the first rule of thumb regarding yachts, whether you are a guest or an owner, is to avoid calling them yachts.

Being a guest on a yacht requires some preparation on your part. First, take appropriate clothes—denims or cottons, rubber-soled shoes, sweaters and jackets even if the weather is warm, and some raingear, if you will be aboard very long.

Second, plan to stow (put away) your gear as soon as you are assigned sleeping quarters. Because of the limited space on a boat, you must be a neat guest. Keep your personal gear out of sight when you are not wearing it, and ask where you are to dispose of paper or other garbage.

If a yacht does not have a crew, be prepared to lend a hand, but only if you are asked. If you do not know how to do something you are asked to do, admit this right away, since trying to perform a task you do not understand could jeopardize the lives of everyone aboard.

If the boat has a crew or is large, this is a sign to you that things are a little more formal. You may wear a suit, if you are a man, to lunch or dinner (always wear a suit if you are invited to dine aboard any large vessel), and women may be expected to wear long dresses to dinner. Check with your host if you have any questions as to the dress that will be expected.

CONDUCTING OTHER BUSINESS ENTERTAINMENT

Caterers and hotel food service managers report that less business entertaining is done at home than in previous years. The major reason, they all felt, was the change in women's roles. When both spouses hold executive positions, the time they spend together is precious and often limited, and they may not be willing to give up an evening at home to entertaining business associates, aside from the traditional bash they throw for the office staff or their colleagues.

As a result, there has been a rise in business entertaining in public places. This requires a great need to be creative in planning the entertainment. There is still traditional entertaining at sports events, where companies give tickets to a football game to prized customers or even entertain them at the game, but there has been an increase in entertainment in conjunction with the arts. A large Chicago bank buys a large block of tickets at Ravinia, an outdoor concert park. They bus their guests out to the park, and the evening begins with an open bar, followed by an elaborate picnic under a tent. Following the concert the guests wind up the evening with drinks and sundaes.

There is little difference between planning an on-premises function and an arts- or sports-oriented function, such as the one just described. Begin by hiring the best and most professional caterer you can find; sit down and work out the budget, entertaining objective, and actual services and food required—then relax and let the caterer handle everything. The executives do function as hosts during the evening, but if anything goes wrong they can talk it over with the service representative who will be on hand to direct the party food and service.

HOSTING A CATERED FUNCTION

There are just a few guidelines to follow if you are an executive or a salesperson representing your company at any official function. One, this is a business function; you may partake of the food and drink, but your interest in it should be downplayed. An executive host with any finesse will never be seen going through the buffet line with everyone else. When everyone is served, he or she may lightly fill a plate with a few tidbits and then circulate among the guests. Salespersons should be forewarned that the same is expected of them. While the atmosphere is soft-sell, there is a purpose to the function, and a salesperson should not see this as a festive occasion in which to eat and drink as much as possible.

Guests, too, should be aware of the gracious way to handle business functions at which food and drinks are served. Always eat lightly—look as if you are paid enough by your own company to eat regularly. Drink lightly, too, so that you are responsive to the business purpose of the function. Never walk up to a bar at a business function and request a double—it is an insult to the host, who has presumably made arrangements for you to be served an adequate-sized drink, to say nothing of being a giveaway to sloppy drinking habits.

Unlike a business entertainment that is obviously purely social (a football game, dinner and ballet, a play, or a holiday party), business entertainments include the intention that some business will be conducted, and a guest should be prepared to participate accordingly. Expect to be shown a new product line or to talk some business.

Finally, invitations to such parties usually state a beginning and ending time. Plan to leave before the party dwindles and definitely take leave before the time stated on the invitation. Again, if the image you want to portray is that of a busy, important person, you should look as if you have someplace else to go. Hangers-on, overeaters, and overdrinkers too often gain an undesirable reputation for being as sloppy in business as they are in their socializing.

PLANNING PURELY SOCIAL ENTERTAINING

Business entertaining becomes social when you see a client or customer whom you like outside work with no business motive whatsoever—or at least this is how most executives interviewed defined these circumstances. Still, every executive interviewed qualified this definition by saying that he or she knew someone whose entire social life consisted of entertaining business friends—surely not a purely motiveless venture except in rare circumstances.

Generally, entertaining of a social nature—apart from big wingdings such as the Super Bowl or an occasional customer's night out at the opera, ballet, or theater—is not that common. You need not feel any pressure to ask a customer and spouse to dine with you—and indeed, it may be viewed as slightly aggressive if you push too far in this direction. Many times, you simply will not be on the same social level as many of your customers, so there is no genuine reason for you to see each other socially except to advance your business relationship.

Occasionally two persons or two couples will find that they do have something in common—golf, theater, a love of eating in fine restaurants. A genuine friendship develops. When this happens, the relationship becomes social; it's even smart not to discuss business on social occasions. You simply relate to each other as good friends who enjoy one another's company. A fine line between business and pleasure always exists, though, so be aware of your motivations in seeing a client or customer socially. It may hurt more in the long run to befriend a customer or client, even if you truly enjoy his or her company. The trend today toward separating business and social life is healthy and probably won't be reversed for a long time—if ever.

CHAPTER 7

Entertaining Moguls
and Others at Home

E NTERTAINING BUSINESS ASSOCIATES in your home forges
closer working ties that are likely to last long after the main
event. International clients are especially eager to be invited to
American homes. Americans are known throughout the world for
their informality, and Europeans and South Americans are especially delighted when they are asked to an American patio party,
buffet dinner, or even a picnic.

Having company is an occasion to bring out your best manners,
cleverest entertainment ideas, and most sparkling tableware. This
does not mean, however, that you can entertain only with china,
crystal, and silverware—if you have none of these things, you can
still entertain using pottery, stainless, and a dose of ingenuity.
While formal dinners are fun and elegant, the days when a boss
must be entertained in that style are long gone. Today's entertaining is personal and much more individual.

PLANNING THE PARTY

Having guests in your home is always a special event, and a

125

certain degree of planning is necessary to make the event go smoothly, regardless of how informally you plan to entertain.

Choosing the Kind of Entertainment

First decide on the type of entertainment that suits you best and that also suits the occasion. Although they are infrequent today, you could plan an elegant, formal sit-down dinner. Less formal entertainments include a circulating buffet, where guests help themselves to food from a buffet table and sit throughout the living area of your house or apartment rather than at one table; a sit-down buffet, where guests serve themselves from a sideboard or table but then sit down at a table to eat; an informal, served, sit-down dinner; and a party which, by definition, may be large or small and may or may not entail the serving of a complete meal. A party menu can easily consist of only drinks and appetizers.

Parties with themes are fun—you don't, for example, have to live in Kentucky to celebrate the Kentucky Derby with mint juleps and ham bisquits. You could also plan a Sunday afternoon Russian tea table; a Chinese banquet; a *ristaffel*, which is a traditional Indonesian meal; or any other meal with an international theme. You can plan a costume party, a come-as-you-are party, or even a party of game playing, although if guests will be expected to participate in any way, it is only thoughtful to alert them to this fact when you extend the invitations. Then, too, remember that you are entertaining adults.

Planning the Guest List

Once you have decided on the type of party to give, write out the guest list—with care. The first thing to consider is the number of persons you can comfortably fit into your house or apartment. If you are planning a large party with very simple food and drinks, a larger number of persons can be accommodated. At a sit-down dinner, the number of persons your table can accommodate becomes the important factor.

Within reason, invite persons who will get along fairly well, particularly when you are mixing social and business friends. Don't use business parties to pay off old social obligations, especially to persons whom you do not find particularly entertaining. If you think someone is a drag, the chances are your business associates won't like him or her either. You should strive for a guest list of persons who will find each other interesting—for business or social reasons. You can, if you like, combine a husband's and a wife's colleagues and business associates at the same party, although you have a greater chance for success if the businesses are the same or related.

ISSUING INVITATIONS

Until recently, invitations were always extended by the wife of a married couple to other wives. Today, the etiquette surrounding invitations has become much less formal, in part because of the large number of single persons in business and also because so many wives have active careers of their own that they simply don't have the time or inclination to maintain the family social calendar. These days invitations are usually extended by whomever feels more comfortable doing so—a man often invites his colleagues and a woman may invite her colleagues.

Business associates are frequently asked to weddings and even anniversaries if the party or reception is large, but invitations to small, personal parties—birthdays, for example—are best extended only to those business associates with whom you have a strong personal relationship.

Most invitations are made by phone today. This is more casual, and it usually produces an immediate response. If you telephone someone to invite them to your home, be sure to mention the time and place, the appropriate dress, and the occasion—if there is a special one—for the party or dinner.

For a large party, it is easier to send written invitations. Again, be sure to include all the facts, such as time, place, date, and occasion.

Some clever printed invitations are available, as are some very nice plain ones, but rather than buying something that is merely cute, write your own invitations on plain white or pastel stationery. Be sure to check postal regulations regarding the size of envelopes that can be sent through the mail before you buy any invitations.

Occasionally, it is a nice gesture to extend a written invitation even to an informal dinner. Use plain personal stationery and write something like the following:

Dear Jane,

Kenneth and I are having a few friends over for a cookout on Saturday, July 10. The dress is casual. I hope you will be able to join us.

Cordially,

Suzanne

For a formal dinner, written invitations are a must. Use plain white cards that are already engraved or plain white paper on which you can hand-letter the invitation.

A formal invitation reads as follows:

Mr. and Mrs. Henry Holt
request the pleasure of
Mr. and Mrs. Jones' company
at dinner in honor of
Emily and Robert Longworth
on Friday, the fifteenth of April
at eight-thirty

RSVP
664 N. Lake Shore Avenue   *Black tie*

Notice that the guests' full names are not written in. Invitations to single or married women may be prefaced by "Miss," "Mrs.," or "Ms."

Occasionally you will extend an invitation to a married couple who use different names or to two persons who are living together but not married. With the married couple there is always the option of using the form above, because the woman's social name is Mrs. Jones, but it is also courteous to a woman who prefers to use her own name or to two persons living together to extend an invitation as follows: "Mr. Jones and Ms. Parkhurst." Alternately, for two cohabiting persons, you could extend two invitations.

An acceptance to a formal dinner is always written this way:

> *Mr. and Mrs. Michael Jones*
> *accept with pleasure*
> *the kind invitation of*
> *Mr. and Mrs. Holt*
> *to dinner on Friday, the fifteenth of April*
> *at eight-thirty*

Such a reply is always written on plain white stationery. A formal regret is written in this way:

> *Ms. Jennifer Henhorn*
> *greatly regrets that a previous engagement*
> *prevents her accepting*
> *Mr. and Mrs. Holt's*
> *kind invitation for dinner*
> *on Friday, the fifteenth of April*

Handling Problems with Invitations

Once in a while someone will fail to respond to an invitation. When this happens, call the person; you have a right to know who is and who is not coming and to make plans accordingly. About one-third to one-half of the persons invited to a large party will be unable to attend, so it is especially important, in order to judge the amount of food and drink to be purchased, to have a fairly accurate estimate of the number attending a party or dinner.

When one of a couple is unable to attend a dinner at the last minute, a problem may arise. If you are the guest and this happens, call the host and explain the situation, saying that you and your spouse or escort will both decline if the absence of one will throw off seating arrangements. A gracious host should encourage the person to attend alone unless the dinner is very formal and the seating arrangements truly would be upset. Otherwise the host should make every possible attempt to accommodate a single guest.

More awkward is the situation in which you have a houseguest and have been invited to attend a party at someone else's home. Call the host and explain that you must decline the invitation because of your guest. If it is convenient, the host can encourage you to come with the guest, but if it is at all inconvenient, the host has every right to let you bow out gracefully. Alternately, you can explain the situation to the guest, help him find something else to do with his time, and go to the party anyway.

Single guests at parties have become quite acceptable in these days when the single population is 40 million strong. Few persons think anything of asking a single man or a single woman to come to a party with or without a date. The invitation to bring a date should always be optional, and no single person should feel pressured to do so. Single persons in turn should realize they now have a responsibility to reciprocate; for many years, single men in particular were so popular at dinner parties that their only responsibilities seemed to be to show up and act polite. But today, many couples have crossed single persons off their invitation lists after extending one too many invitations without seeing any signs of reciprocation.

If you are living with someone and your boss or the person giving the party knows this and does not extend an invitation, you cannot take this person with you to the party or dinner any more than you can show up with any unexpected guest. Socially, you may decide not to see persons who do not invite you out as a couple, but in your business relations, it is better to go alone than to bring along an uninvited person. Generally, though, when a couple lives together and this is widely known, they are invited to most functions as a couple.

HOSTING THE LARGE PARTY

Big parties, if handled properly, require time and money. They are best planned far in advance, and they are ideally planned with the aid of a caterer or, at a minimum, a bartender. You can always ask a friend to play bartender to as many as ten persons for a couple of rounds of drinks, but it is an imposition to ask someone to prepare drinks all night for thirty or forty persons. As a general rule, one professional bartender is required for every twenty-five guests. If you are also hiring servers or maids, there should be one for every twenty-five people. Often a caterer will supply persons to work at the party in addition to providing the food (see the section on using a caterer for home entertaining).

The menu for a large party often consists of drinks and appetizers. At a more elaborate party, a simple supper may be served at some point during the evening, but usually the larger the party, the simpler the food.

Once a menu has been worked out and the budget planned, contact a caterer or service agency to arrange for help. A skilled cook can prepare food for any number of persons if he or she really has a mind to do so, but a party of more than thirty persons is easier to handle if a caterer arranges for the food and service. This frees you to be a gracious host—an especially important factor in business entertaining. Decide also whether you will need to rent any supplies such as flatware, glassware, dishes, tables, chairs, or linens. For example, for fifty persons, you will need approximately eighty glasses. This may sound like a lot, but they will all be used throughout the evening. If you plan to do a lot of large-scale entertaining, it may be worthwhile to invest in some inexpensive glasses, but such items are also easily rented. While checking supplies, don't overlook serving dishes and utensils, which can also be rented or borrowed.

Obtaining Bar Supplies

Here is a list of bar accessories necessary for a large party:

tablecloth
cocktail shakers and martini pitchers
water pitcher
bottle openers
ice bucket or other container for ice
jigger measures
corkscrew
bar strainer
teaspoon
long spoon for mixing and stirring
cocktail-sized paper napkins
linen or cloth dish towels
ingredients for special drinks: lemon peel, orange and lemon
    slices, cherries, olives, cocktail onions, bitters, limes, sugar

For a party of fifty you will need the following quantities of liquor:

4 or 5 fifths Scotch

4 or 5 fifths vodka and/or gin
4 or 5 fifths each bourbon, rye, and rum
6 bottles dry white wine (or sherry or aperitif wine)
5 or 6 large bottles each soda water, ginger ale, and tonic
   water
12 bottles Perrier or other good bottled water
12 small bottles soft drinks

Buy ice at the same time you buy the liquor. When buying liquor in quantity, ask the liquor dealer for a discount and make arrangements to return any unopened bottles. If a dealer won't permit this, shop for a new merchant.

Planning the Menu

When preparing the food, at least do yourself the favor of serving foods that can be prepared in advance and served with ease. Chips, nuts, and *crudités* with a good sauce can obviously be prepared in advance. Stuffed eggs or mushrooms can be partially prepared, although they should be stuffed the day of the party. Cocktail sandwiches, small quiches, and tiny cream puffs can all be made in advance and kept refrigerated (covered with a damp towel) until serving time. Anything spread on toast or crackers is liable to get soggy and so should be prepared at the last minute.

Preparing the House

Clean house well in advance — and it should be sparkling. That is a compliment to your guests. Glasses that are not used frequently may need to be washed, and silver will surely need polishing. The evening before the party is a good time to rearrange any furniture to accommodate the large number of guests. Several days before the party make a check to be sure there are enough matches, ash trays, candles, fresh soap, bathroom tissue, paper coasters, cigarettes, and guest towels.

If you are planning to have a centerpiece made up by a florist, it should be ordered in advance and scheduled for delivery early on the day of the party.

On the day of the party, you will only have to set up the bar, set the table where food will be served, and make last-minute preparations of food. Try to have everything done by late afternoon so you can take a few hours to relax and get ready. Immediately before the guests arrive, set out the food and the ice.

Greeting Your Guests

You are now ready to greet your guests. Meet each one at the door, take the coats or tell them where they may put them, and then usher the new arrivals into the room of the party and make at least one introduction so newcomers will have someone to talk with immediately.

At a big party, unlike at a dinner or smaller entertainment, there may be some stayers-on until the wee hours. Although subtle and even not-so-subtle hints can be dropped at a small dinner party to let guests know it is time to depart, part of giving a large party seems to be taking care of the hangers-on. While it is perfectly all right to cut off the drinks at a certain point, it is an especially warm gesture to be prepared to send late-stayers on their way with a last round of food. Scrambled eggs and coffee are the traditional standbys.

HOSTING THE BUFFET DINNER

There are two kinds of buffet dinners. In each the food is put out on a table or sideboard and the guests help themselves. In one kind of buffet, the guests seat themselves as they would at any informal sit-down dinner; at the other the guests mingle or sit on chairs, sofas, or in any convenient place (including the floor). At the latter kind of dinner, the food must be of a kind that can be eaten with only a fork. With either kind of buffet, the food can be fairly simple: one or two hearty main dishes, salad, cheeses, and dessert. The only pieces of special serving equipment needed for a buffet dinner are warming trays that will keep the food hot.

If you are not planning a sit-down buffet, be sure there are enough chairs (and small tables, if you can manage it), so that everyone can sit down somewhere while eating. At this kind of buffet, the dining room table is often the best place to serve the meal. The drawing that follows shows the proper way to set a table for a buffet dinner.

The main thing to remember in setting a buffet table is that everything should be organized for the convenience of the guests. They will naturally need to pick up their plates and flatware first. Serving platters should be arranged in such a way as to help the flow of traffic rather than impede it.

Serving the Dinner

When the guests arrive, offer mixed drinks or wine and give everyone a little time to settle in. You may want to have bowls of nuts, olives, or other tidbits around for guests to nibble on early in the evening.

When all the hot food has been placed on the table, announce that dinner is served. If the meal is being catered and there are waiters, they will help serve the guests. If you are without help, be prepared to cut pieces of cheese for guests or offer them dessert— anything to facilitate their progress.

Plan to serve main dishes that each guest can serve himself or herself using a spoon. After everyone has been served, replace covers on dishes and return them to the oven if necessary. To offer seconds, bring the dishes back to the table or, if convenient, ask guests whether you can take their plates and refill them. When each person finishes eating, remove the dishes. Dessert can be served right away, or you may prefer to wait a while. The interlude between the main part of the meal and dessert is a good time to clean ash trays and set out coffee and dessert dishes.

At a seated buffet, tables and chairs are provided for each guest. Don't forget that it is possible to borrow or rent card tables, thus allowing you to use your dining table for serving food. Chairs need not match, and unity can be created with tablecloths of the same fabric, centerpieces and candles that carry out a color theme, and dishes that match or coordinate. At a seated buffet, put the first course on the table before the guests are seated. If there are waiters, they can remove these plates while the guests help themselves to food at the buffet table. Waiters can also pass rolls and sauces and offer second helpings to the guests. The dishes will need to be cleared after the main course. Dessert can be served from the buffet or brought to the seated guests, as can coffee.

A buffet table, as well as a dinner table, is often enhanced with a centerpiece. Although flowers are traditional, there is no reason to be limited to them. An absolutely lovely centerpiece can be made from fresh vegetables in a basket; a bowl filled with lemons is stunning. There is really no end to the inventive ideas that can be put to work in a centerpiece. If flowers are ordered, be sure to purchase a low arrangement, especially at a sit-down dinner, so the guests do not have to dodge the centerpiece to talk with one another. Candles are always a nice touch at a company meal, and they go beautifully with flowers. If the table is already crowded with food, however, skip the centerpiece; it is not a necessity.

Making a Checklist for a Buffet Dinner

Here are checklists for the equipment needed for a buffet supper:

Drinks

> glasses
> wine, liquor and soft drinks, bottled water
> cocktail shakers and pitchers
> ice
> bottle openers and corkscrew
> olives, lemons, limes, onions, and so on
> napkins and coasters

Dinner

> enough plates to serve everyone with every course
> wine glasses
> tablecloths, place mats, and napkins

food-warming equipment
salts and peppers, other condiments
ash trays
sugar bowl and creamer
coffee cups and after-dinner drink glasses
extra tables and chairs if it is a sit-down meal

Miscellaneous

cigarettes
matches
guest towels
extra ash trays
centerpiece
candles

HOSTING THE INFORMAL DINNER

An informal dinner is not much harder to manage than a buffet. The number of persons invited depends upon the number that can be seated at your table; or again, you might rent small tables. If small tables are used, make sure they all seat the same number of persons. Nothing is guaranteed to make a guest feel slighted faster than being seated at a table that makes the guest look less honored than others, as happens, for example, when six persons are seated at one table and eight are divided between two small tables.

At an informal dinner, a tablecloth or individual place mats can be used, but a tablecloth tends to unify the table, make it look less cluttered, and give it a festive appearance. The drawing here shows how to set a table for a sit-down dinner.

Sit-down dinner

Perfectionists, take note: there is even an etiquette to putting flatware on the table. It goes as follows: all flatware should be lined up at its bottom edge; the blade of the knife should turn inward; the tines of the fork go up; all flatware should be placed about an inch from the table edge. The flatware that will be used first is placed farthest from the plate. Remember that the salad fork should go inside the dinner fork if you are planning to serve salad after the entrée; otherwise, put it on the outside.

If you are having a large seated dinner for more than eight persons, it is nice to have separate condiments, butters, and salt and pepper shakers for each end of the table. The one exception is a peppermill. Since so many people today have cultivated a taste for fresh-ground pepper, and since food tastes so much better with it, by all means pass the peppermill if you have one and dispense with individual pepper shakers.

Making a Checklist for an Informal Dinner

Here is a basic checklist for an informal dinner:

place mats, tablecloth or runners, and napkins
plates for all courses
flatware for all courses
wine and water glasses
coffee cups, dessert plates, and after-dinner drink glasses
candles
centerpiece
ash trays, cigarettes, and matches
salt and pepper shakers, butter dishes, condiments
serving dishes
serving flatware
coasters for wine bottles or carafe
trivets for hot dishes

Serving an Informal Dinner

Food can be served from the kitchen or it can be served from a sideboard, whichever is more convenient. Since there is a great deal of effort involved in serving this kind of meal, if you will be serving it without help, try to prepare simple dishes that require only minimal last-minute finishing.

You will probably want to serve drinks and possibly an appetizer as the guests arrive. Generally an informal meal is served anywhere from thirty to sixty minutes after the time on the invitation. Latecomers at a dinner party are fairly inexcusable, since there is every chance that food cannot be held over past a certain length of time, so if someone doesn't arrive by the time the food is ready, eat without them. This may sound discourteous to the latecomers, but it is, in fact, very courteous to those who arrived at the appointed time and who have a right to eat food when it is at its peak. Guests who show up when a meal is in progress should make quick apologies to the host, seat themselves without fuss, and take up at whatever course everyone else is eating.

Put soup or any other first course on the table just before dinner is announced. Clear the first course and then bring out the main course. Wine is poured with each course. Be sure to bring out the rolls when the main course is served.

The manner of serving at an informal dinner varies depending upon the part of the country one lives in and how formal one's social group is. In small communities dishes are often put on the table and then passed family-style. Meat is often carved in the kitchen and sometimes the plates are filled there and brought to the table. In New York and Chicago food is more likely to be ceremoniously carved at the table, and the host may fill each plate and then pass it to the guests. In either case, a sideboard may be set up to serve from rather than making numerous jaunts back and forth to the kitchen. An informal dinner can be juggled by one person, but is considerably easier for a couple to handle. One person can serve while the other clears. One person can offer seconds while the other readies the coffee and dessert.

If the dinner is very large and is being catered, waiters will, of course, do the serving. Even for a smaller dinner party of six to ten persons, it is sometimes helpful to hire someone to help with the serving. Discuss with servers in detail what you will expect from them and write up a list to post in the kitchen. Work out what each of you will do—you will serve the soup, while the helper passes the crackers; the helper will clear the drink glasses from the living room while everyone eats the main course; the helper will offer seconds to everyone while they are seated. What you expect from a helper is not so important as the fact that you have worked it all out in advance so the meal will go smoothly. Ten persons is probably the most that one person or a couple who are hosting a dinner can serve without having the meal take on the aura of a three-ring circus. A single hired server should not be expected to handle more than twelve persons.

A word of warning, though: when in a company town, do as the company people do. You may have just been transplanted from a sophisticated Boston or New York milieu where no one thinks anything of being served by a maid even at a small informal dinner. In your new community, a maid serving dinner to so few may be considered putting on airs. In some towns and small cities, serving meals in courses rather than passing the food family-style is considered pompous. While everyone should be open to new dining experiences whenever possible, for business entertainment, the risk may be too great. Your closest friends may be delighted to be asked to a formal dinner party the likes of which they have never seen before, but your colleagues may feel they are being subjected to an ostentatious show of power. So before you launch into any unusual or highly formal modes of entertaining, take the pulse of your guests and community.

Hosting the Formal Dinner

Black-tie dinners are rarely held these days except for official entertaining in Washington, D.C., or at the United Nations, but a special occasion calling for one may arise: an important European guest is visiting your company, an important business merger is being celebrated, or someone important within the company is celebrating something.

Formal dinners call for formal written invitations, as noted in the section on invitations. They are invariably black tie. A formal dinner always consists of several courses. Although the number may vary, four or five is the usual number served today. Several wines are served: white wines first with the fish course and a red wine or different white wine with the entrée. Two is the usual number of wines served, although three may be required depending upon the food.

While you can do your own cooking at a formal dinner, you

cannot do your own serving. Since you will hire a caterer or service agency to help you, be sure to check references before hiring to assure yourself that the caterer is trained to handle a formal dinner. This is not the time to skimp on the caterer or service personnel; hire the very best you can afford. One waiter or waitress is required for every six to eight guests.

Setting the Table

A formal dinner calls for good china, silverware, white table linens, candles and a centerpiece, usually of flowers. Place cards are always used to indicate where guests sit. They go in the center above the plate and are handwritten in this form: "Mr. Brown," "Ms. Stettler," or "Mrs. Linden." If there are two Browns, write "Mr. James Brown" and "Mr. Everett Brown."

Greeting the Guests

Guests are expected to arrive promptly for a formal dinner because there is usually a guest of honor, and he or she is not supposed to walk into an empty room. A guest of honor who knows his or her etiquette will also take care to leave first, although other guests who have a special reason to do so may of course leave whenever they have to, and the rules have softened considerably on this in recent years. Dinner is served within thirty minutes of the arrival of the guest of honor.

Entering the Dining Room

There is a ritual for entering the dining room at a formal dinner. The host offers his arm to the woman guest of honor and the hostess is escorted in by the male guest of honor. Other guests can escort each other in as they see fit, but at truly formal dinners, one is likely either to encounter a seating chart or (in the case of male guests) to be handed a small envelope at the door telling each the name of the woman he is expected to escort in. (Only at a formal dinner does having an even number of guests become a necessity.)

The female guest of honor usually sits to the right of the host, and the male guest of honor to the right of the hostess.

Proposing Toasts

Toasts are commonly made at a formal dinner, although they are appropriate at any time that good friends have gathered. At a formal dinner, the host offers the first toast to the guest of honor. It should be short and flattering. Everyone except the person being toasted drinks, even nondrinkers, who may raise an empty wine glass or water glass. The person being toasted is expected to respond. The shortest and perhaps most appreciated response is to stand, raise your glass to those who toasted you, and say, "Thank you." More can be said, but remember that a toast is not a speech. Once the initial toast has been made by the host or hostess, anyone is free to offer additional ones.

Separating Men and Women After Dinner

At the end of the meal, everyone leaves the dining room in the same way that they entered, that is, escorting the same person. Until recently men and women usually separated for a brief period of time at this point, the men to have drinks and cigars, the women presumably to catch up on subjects of interest only to them. If you are attending a formal dinner in Washington or at the United Nations, this still occurs, but in most homes, there is no longer so arbitrary a separation of the sexes.

Another problem sometimes arises at any kind of dinner party, though, and that is the unintentional separation of men and women. Too often the women congregate in the kitchen to discuss their children and the men (and perhaps the women who have fascinating careers) congregate elsewhere, invariably to discuss work. Almost everyone who attends these evenings finds them boring. It is up to the host to bring persons back together or to say to one group, "Why don't we join the others?" But there is also a responsibility of each guest to mingle with everyone at a party. Parties, however large or small, are festive occasions, and everyone present should put forth his or her best effort to create a festive atmosphere.

Serving Drinks

Whenever people gather socially, drinks are inevitably a part of the evening, although in recent years there has been a trend away from serving mixed drinks toward serving aperitif wines. Most persons will want to be prepared for any requests.

Before serving anything, though, you will need an adequate selection of glasses. Only you can decide what kind of investment you want to make in these, in terms of cash and in terms of the quality you think you will need. Inexpensive dimestore glasses work very well, especially for those extra sets of glasses that are only brought out a couple of times a year for a large party. Although there are specially-shaped glasses for white and red wine, you can buy one all-purpose glass in which you can serve any kind of wine, sherry, and even champagne. You can also buy the elegant tapered champagne glasses that are meant to be used only for the bubbly, and the cavernous glasses in which brandy is served.

A well-stocked bar might include Scotch, bourbon, rye or blended whiskey, gin, and vodka. Today it also usually includes a dry sherry, a couple of aperitif wines, and vermouth. For mixes and those who do not drink alcohol, have a selection of soft drinks, soda water, a good bottled water, and tonic water.

The following chart shows the number of predinner drinks you can expect to serve. It is only a guide, and the amounts suggested are on the ample side.

Number of Persons	Number of Predinner Drinks	Liquor
4	8 to 16	1 fifth
6	12 to 24	2 fifths
8	16 to 24	2 fifths
12	24 to 48	3 fifths
20	40 to 75	4 fifths

The number of drinks served at any social gathering is fairly easy to control. Simply cut off the predinner drinking—and do the guests' taste buds a favor—by announcing that dinner is served. At the end of the evening when it is time to wrap everything up, stop offering drinks.

The varieties of mixed drinks that can be served are too vast to list here and can be obtained from any good book on the subject, but there are a few things to know about mixing drinks in general. Always measure ingredients exactly, using a jigger, which is 1½ ounces; a pony, which is ¾ ounce; or a bar spoon, which is ½ teaspoon. A dash means 8 to 10 drops of something. Drinks that contain eggs, fruit juice, and other ingredients of a texture that is different from the liquor should be shaken vigorously to ensure thorough mixing. Drinks with carbonated beverages should never be shaken but should be stirred.

Start mixing any drink by putting ice in the glass, and always put fresh ice in every drink when you offer another round.

Use granulated sugar to sweeten drinks, but when you are serving a lot of people, it is easier to premix a syrup of ½ pound of sugar in ¾ cup of boiling water.

Serving Wines

Wines are easier to serve than are mixed drinks, since they only need uncorking and pouring. Selecting the right wine to go with a food, however, is an art. The best way to learn about wines is to befriend a knowledgeable wine merchant, take his or her advice about what to buy, and drink, drink, drink until you have developed a palate that tells you what wines are fine and what foods they complement.

Generally red wines go with red meat and other foods that are hearty except seafood and fish. White wines go with fish and seafood, some veal dishes (others are enhanced by reds), and light dishes that simply would be overpowered by a red. Sweet wines are served only with sweet foods, and they are meant to be served after dry wines. White wines are served before red wines.

There is a great deal of mostly misinformed debate about the best temperature for serving wines. Generally it is said that white wines should be served chilled and red wines should be served at room temperature. The catch is that the room temperature that is best for a red is wine cellar temperature—55 to 68 degrees Fahrenheit. So when serving a red wine, chill it slightly. One apartment dweller we know puts red wines on a windowsill for a while before serving. Others chill the wine in the refrigerator for about thirty minutes before uncorking it. Red wines should be uncorked an hour or so before serving to allow them to breathe. After opening a bottle of wine, always smell the cork for any sign of sourness; this means the wine has begun to turn to vinegar and should not be drunk. Save it for salad dressing!

Wine glasses are placed to the right of the water glass. The wine glass closest to the water glass is the first one used. If more than one wine is served during a meal, the empty wine glass is removed with each course. Pour wines at the beginning of each course, and do not lift the glass from the table to pour the wine. Fill the glass about half-full, so the wine can expand in the glass and the drinker can inhale the full aroma before sipping.

Numerous countries produce their own wines, and more and more of these are being imported into the United States. It is fun to experiment with these wines at tasting parties, but when you are serving a dinner that has taken effort and time to prepare, try to buy a wine that complements the food. Here is a general guideline:

Appetizers, cheeses, canapés: Sherry, vermouth, champagne, or any of the white aperitif wines.

Poultry: Rhine wine, dry sauterne, white burgundy, or white bordeaux.

Seafood: Chablis, Rhine wine, moselle, white burgundy, or dry sauterne.

Beef or hearty or red-sauced dishes: Red burgundy, red bordeaux.

Veal and ham: Red or white bordeaux or a white burgundy.

Eggs: Light red or dry white wine such as you might serve with fish.

Desserts: Port, sweet sherry, muscatel, or sweet sauterne.

After dinner or with coffee: Brandy, any of the various sweet after-dinner liqueurs, such as Benedictine or crème de menthe.

HIRING A CATERER FOR HOME ENTERTAINING

Although many persons are familiar with what is termed semicatering—having trays of food brought in by a caterer for a large party—fewer persons are aware of the full range of services a fine caterer can offer for at-home business entertaining. Caterers can serve an elegant formal dinner for six members of the board of directors or for eighteeen of your top executives—and many chairpersons and company presidents occasionally do opt for such a gala occasion. A caterer can serve a stand-up buffet or even plan a large party at which you pay off all the business obligations you have accumulated throughout the year.

In full catering, and this is probably what you will need and want for business entertaining, the caterer can furnish everything—the dishes, chairs, tables, waiters, bartenders, chef, and of course, the food—or the caterer may use your dishes and silver according to your preference.

Contact several top-notch caterers and choose one. The quality of caterers varies greatly, and while hiring a mom-and-pop group for a small party may work, only a professional caterer can guarantee you the smooth-running operation you will want for a business party. A professional caterer also provides a complete package—and best of all, will clean up afterwards, something many smaller caterers won't do. By all means, check a caterer's references; ask for names of present and former clients and then call them. Or ask a friend who entertains a lot who can be trusted to handle the kind of party you want.

Once you have found one or two caterers who are possibilities (even in large cities, there are usually only two or three truly professional organizations), make appointments to talk with their service representatives. The most important thing to establish in these meetings is your budget. It is a waste of your time and the caterer's if you decide to listen to the most elaborate entertaining package they can offer and then announce two hours into the meeting that you can only afford to spend $12 per person. A qualified, professional caterer is willing to work within your budget, but he or she cannot do so until you have made clear what that budget is.

Explain the purpose of the party or dinner. Are you entertaining three of your most important clients and their wives and husbands? Are you entertaining international visitors? Is this your annual backyard bash for your employees? Ask the caterer to come to your home to see the facilities. Together draw up a list of the equipment to be rented. Have the size of the guest list in mind before the first meeting with the service representative, so you can talk in specific terms.

Caterers provide a cook, if that is what is called for, as well as bartenders and any other servers that are necessary. Persons who work for professional caterers are often homemakers, unemployed actors, artists, or writers, college students, and persons who recently emigrated to the United States from Europe and were in service there, so as a general rule, there will be little problem with the service personnel. If you have any specific requests, such as asking that the bartender not joke with the guests, explain this politely to the representative when planning the party or dinner. In fact, any personal preferences should be explained in advance so the person who manages your party can make sure that your wishes are met by giving advance instructions to the personnel. This person or some other managerial representative of the caterer will undoubtedly attend the party, and this provides a nice buffer between you and any problems that may arise with service, food, use of facilities, or clean-up responsibilities.

The caterer should be expected to clean up after a party, but ask in advance and make sure this is included in the written contract. And by all means get a written contract from the caterer, and ask before you sign whether it is all-inclusive, that is, whether there will be any extra charges.

Few caterers supply liquor or wine, so you will have to negotiate your own deal for this with the liquor or wine merchant. A caterer may be able to suggest someone reliable who will also give you good service. There is a case discount of 10 percent, and most liquor dealers will let you return unopened bottles. If your dealer refuses, shop around a little more.

Kathy Dieckmann, the knowledgeable sales manager at Gaper's, the largest and best-known caterer in Chicago, said that anyone hiring a caterer should have a long list of questions to ask before finalizing the deal:

Will food be prepared on premises?
What grade of meat will be served?
Will the vegetables be fresh?
Where will food be prepared?
How will food be prepared?
How many servers and personnel will be involved?
How many carving stations will be used?
Will there be long lines at the buffet?
Will there be long lines at the dinner?
Will they pour both red and white wines in case persons want
   both?
Will they charcoal-broil beef?
Will they be able to serve coffee before dessert if someone
   requests it?

A good caterer should be able to answer these and any other
questions that any good host would ask of himself or herself while
planning a party.

As for the menu itself, when working out a meal with a caterer,
you should have a few suggestions or ideas about the kind of food
you prefer to serve to guests. A caterer's consultant will also have
many suggestions, and a professional caterer can prepare almost
anything (the limitations are usually your kitchen, not the caterer's cooking skill), but it helps if you know what you want.

BEING THE HOST

Throughout this chapter, the word "host" has usually been
used to refer to either a man or a woman who is entertaining
guests; it is less awkward than "host or hostess." Except where
specific references are being made to women, we shall continue to
use "host" throughout this chapter except for those few cases
where the distinctions are more clearly drawn.

A host (male or female) has only one true responsibility: the guests. The entire event is planned for their enjoyment, and everything possible must be done to make them feel welcome in your home and to ensure that they have a pleasant evening.

Begin by being ready and waiting for company. Few things hit a more sour note than greeting guests (especially the first ones, who find arriving first a bit awkward in itself) with the message that you are not quite ready for them and then letting them sit in the living room alone while you complete last-minute personal and cooking preparations. Go to the door when guests arrive, shake hands, and say how happy you are to see them. This cordiality is appropriate even if you saw the guest a few hours ago at work.

Although the days of abundant social kissing appear to have let up somewhat (in many places), some persons still think this is the appropriate greeting, and if you are the host and someone appears ready to make this gesture, it is only gracious to reciprocate. On the other hand, it is a warm and natural gesture to greet old friends with a kiss and a hug, regardless of who else is present.

Take guests' coats or show them where they can hang them. Notice the word "hang." If at all possible, plan a way to hang up coats; clear out the front hall closet temporarily or rent or buy a portable coat hanger.

Making Introductions

Escort guests into the living room. If the party is small, new arrivals should be introduced to everyone. At a large party, introduce them to one or two couples or a group standing nearby and then excuse yourself to greet other guests. Since first names are so commonly used today, most introductions, with a few exceptions, are made with first and last names. If you are introducing someone very much older to someone young, it is still courteous to use "Mr.," "Mrs.," or "Ms." Be careful about this, however, when guests are business associates. You never want to accord the status of wise elder to someone who will be offended by it, such as a very powerful man or woman who may indeed be older than his or her subordinates but has no desire to acknowledge this. Ministers, rabbis, priests, and higher-ranking Catholic clergy, senators, and others above that rank, including judges, are often introduced using their titles, especially if the individual is the guest of honor. Medical doctors, dentists, and persons with doctorates do not use their titles socially. You will quite naturally want to identify a relative, but avoid qualifying any other introduction except where necessary to start a conversation. Don't say, for example: "This is Jack Johnson, my very good friend." It is assumed that any guest in your home is a very good friend. It is tactful to say, "This is Jack Johnson. He was my college roommate and is in town from Cincinnati for a few days." Or if you know two persons are going to have difficulty starting a conversation, you might add something such as, "Myra just got promoted to account executive at O'Grady Advertising," or "Jeff and Cindy just returned from a food tour of France."

Introducing two people who are living together to other guests often produces a moment of awkwardness; it need not. Simply introduce the persons by their names and omit any reference to their relationship. A similar situation often occurs when a married couple use two surnames; again, simply introduce the persons by their names and let later conversation turn up how the persons are related to one another.

When several guests have arrived and are seated, don't vanish to the kitchen if you can possibly avoid doing so, for your departure almost guarantees an awkward lull in the conversation except among very old friends. Stay for a while and keep the conversation rolling.

On the other hand, a host should always be subtle in manipulating a conversation. No guest wants to feel that he or she is being given the third degree, and some persons, especially writers and artists, are shy about discussing their work. Politicians and newspaper reporters, on the other hand, are almost always gregarious, and your task may be to keep them from monopolizing the conversation—or the entire evening, for that matter.

Give guests room to open up in their own ways. No one appreciates a host who says, "Jack is going to tell us about his trip to Greece now." If someone needs to be brought out, do it quietly, possibly in a two- or three-way conversation; a shy person won't be eager to be the center of attention anyway. If someone needs to be stopped, do take advantage of even the smallest lull to turn to someone else and say, "Not to change the subject, but what did you enjoy most about your visit to Costa Rica, Sally?"

The host is responsible for seating arrangements at a dinner. At a formal dinner, this is all planned in advance (see the section on formal dinners), but for informal dinners the host may use place cards or may simply indicate where each of the guests is to sit when he or she enters the dining room.

A guest of honor, however unofficial—an out-of-town visitor, an old college friend, a long-lost cousin—may be accorded the place of honor if there are no official guests of honor. When business associates are present, the highest-ranking one (like your boss!) is given the place of honor. Seating is frequently more interesting when men and women alternate, although this is not a hard and fast rule. Try to separate persons who see each other frequently and mix those who have just met.

A very good ploy with dull or shy persons is to put them together. A shy person is often bowled over by an outgoing, aggressive person and will become even quieter, while two shy persons often bring each other out beautifully.

If you are serving the meal yourself, as is usually the case at informal dinners today, excuse yourself quietly when you must leave the table. Do not let others pop up to help you, no matter how persistently they offer. Remember that you are expected to take the first bite of any course, so don't serve the soup and then vanish into the kitchen to pull the roast out of the oven. It's never appropriate to suggest that your guests start without you—somehow a gracious guest is just too aware of the trouble taken in preparing a special meal and wants the cook to take the traditional first bite.

Until the 1940s, a host was expected to "turn the table" midway during the dinner. This was often done quite abruptly, by turning from one's partner on one side and saying to the person seated on the other side, "Now I'm going to talk to you." Every person at the table followed suit in pretty short order. Fortunately that slightly rude custom has given way to a more gracious one in which everyone present at a dinner table talks at some point to the person on either side whenever it is comfortable during the meal.

A meal is officially over when the last person has finished eating dessert. Coffee can be served at the table, but it is more often served in the living room, and guests are usually ready to move around after a heavy meal anyway. Shortly after the last person has finished eating dessert or during a lull in the conversation, the host should stand, a signal to the guests that everyone is going to move away from the table.

Handling Guests' Departures

There are no longer any formal rules about when a guest leaves a dinner or a party. Of course, a party is expected to run late, particularly if it is held on a weekend night. After a dinner party, guests usually linger an hour or an hour and a half over coffee and brandy. If the conversation is scintillating, there is nothing to keep a party or dinner from going on for hours. When a guest does want to leave, he or she simply stands and says goodbye, complimenting the host on the food or the company or both.

It is gracious for the host to say, "Oh, must you really leave now? We've enjoyed seeing you so much," but this is a mere formality. Departing guests still are expected to depart. The guests thank the host again at the door and the host thanks them again for coming. Escort guests to the door or to an elevator. Old persons may even be escorted to their car, particularly if the hour is late. Most guests who are going to call a taxi will ask where the telephone is and do it themselves, but if they are not familiar with the community, it is helpful to call one for them. Try to keep goodbyes with the first guests brief so other guests don't think they are being signaled to leave, too.

Single women frequently come and go unescorted today, particularly in large cities, but most hosts will show some concern for how a woman alone is getting home late at night. If possible, ask another guest to drive her or call a cab for her if the hour is very late.

Those who have drunk too much may require a little help getting home and this can be especially tricky when dealing with business associates. No one wants to be in the position of telling an important client or boss that he or she cannot safely drive home, but the situation just may arise. Try to avoid long-winded arguments over the issue. If possible, just assume that the person will not be driving his or her own car home. Call a taxi and then tell the person what you have done. Better yet, ask someone else to take the overimbiber home and tell him or her discreetly that you will bring the car over the next day or wait for it to be picked up. Assume that the person knows he or she will not be driving home under the circumstances.

Some guests, unfortunately, do not know when to leave, and a wise host or hostess needs a few signals for such occasions. First, stop serving drinks. Second, let a lull in the conversation hang. If you constantly jump in with new topics to keep the evening alive, your guests may never take the hint and go home. As a last resort, start to clear glasses and ash trays while still talking to your guests. If all else fails, you will have to say something. Make it sound as if you would like the party to go on for days were it not for the fact that you have to meet a plane at 6 A.M. the next day or get up at 5 A.M. to finish a report. You need not even say this directly to a guest; just comment off-handedly that you wish you didn't have "that darned report" to finish tomorrow.

HANDLING CHILDREN AT A PARTY

Generally when you are involved in business entertaining, your children should not be present, even for dinner. They may, if you wish, come into the party or dinner when it is just beginning to meet the guests.

If you have very small children, you may want to hire a babysitter to take care of them so you do not constantly have to break away to handle their requests.

DETERMINING THE PRICE OF ENTERTAINING

Ticklish moments often occur when a guest spills a drink or otherwise damages something or breaks a valuable or cherished object. Think of this as the ultimate test of your poise. Even if you want to put your hands around the person's neck and squeeze, act as if the incident were nothing. What is one less piece of Boehm china? The white sofa needed to be cleaned anyway. You always were superstitious about having an even-numbered set of antique crystal sherry glasses.

As for the guest's responsibility, profuse apologies are, of course, in order, but there is more to be done. If the object is not of great value or is not too rare to be replaced, another should be obtained. A guest who breaks a wine glass or china plate should send a replacement to the host as soon as possible, along with a brief note apologizing again for the accident. If something truly precious has been broken that the guest obviously cannot replace, the breaker should still send a gift by way of apology. If your budget is modest, flowers, a book, or candy will work nicely, again accompanied by a note. If you can afford a nicer present—

not a replacement, but something lovely to compensate—send it along.

If you have damaged something, try to make arrangements for its repair. Most hosts will refuse to let you do this if you state your intentions, so discretion is called for. First check with your insurance agent the morning after a party to see whether your insurance will pay for damages; if so, ask an adjustor to call on the host and discuss the repairs needed. If you have burned a hole in a table or spilled something on a piece of furniture, call an expert and make arrangements for him or her to see the host to discuss repairs. Make it clear to the supplier that you expect to pay the bill and that it is not even to be discussed with the host. Since most persons do start to seethe quietly (or otherwise) the morning after the party when they get another look at the burn in the coffee table or the liquor stain on the sofa, they are usually quite delighted to see someone who plans to repair their property, regardless of how much they may protest to you that the courtesy is unnecessary.

WELCOMING UNEXPECTED GUESTS

Uninvited and unannounced guests are rare, but they sometimes appear. At an open house, an extra body is of no consequence, but at a dinner party, it can be deadly. If someone is actually rude enough to simply arrive with an uninvited guest, a gracious host should first of all try to make room for him or her. If there is no place to seat the person or if there truly will not be enough food, tell the person who has brought the guest that while you would love to have him or her stay, it simply isn't possible. Tell them exactly why it is impossible, too (no extra chair, not enough food), so your refusal will not appear to be a mere ploy you are using because you are annoyed.

On the other hand, if someone has called in advance and you have both agreed that the extra guest is welcome, it is thoughtful to write or telephone the extra guest to extend a personal invitation.

CHOOSING APPROPRIATE DRESS

For a woman, one of the joys of entertaining is that you can wear your most stunning clothes—you can even coordinate your at-home clothes with your household color scheme, if you are so inclined. You do need to dress for the occasion, whatever it may be. No other woman appreciates a hostess who has told her guests to wear jeans when she herself appears in a stunning pair of evening pajamas. When the boss or important business associates are coming to dinner, one reservation should be kept in mind—the same one that would apply were that person entertaining you— dress down a little bit. Flamboyance in a company that does not cherish this trait could hurt more than it helps, even if it occurs in your home. The same thing applies with regard to local community standards of dress. If everyone generally wears casual clothes to parties and dinners, your annual black-tie dinner may be enjoyed, but giving a black-tie dinner every two months will only be considered putting on airs. As in other areas of business, there are times when it is more advantageous to fit in—and this is probably one of those times.

A final word about having important executives to dinner: relax and enjoy yourself. The guests will come ready to have fun, and if you are ready to entertain graciously, there is no reason for a party or dinner to be anything other than a stunning success.

CHAPTER 8

The ABCs of Eating
and Drinking

TABLE MANNERS? Surely they don't belong in a book about getting ahead? After all, don't education, skills, contacts, personality—anything else, for that matter—count more? It is true that these other things are vitally important, but make no mistake about it, how you handle the task of putting food in your mouth is a very big part of your image—professional and social.

Business executives who have already made it to the top frequently lament the lack of social polish in their protégés—and one of the first places where rough edges show up is at the table.

Ironically, to someone who was taught correct manners from the cradle, using good table manners is second nature and not even something one spends time worrying about. Yet such persons— the same persons whose family or educational contacts give them a headstart in the race to the boardroom—do indeed notice how others eat. Even if you don't do something absurdly gauche—such as slurping your soup—those who know enough to break up a piece of bread before eating it will notice someone who doesn't. It is not simply that no one wants to eat with a slob; lack of table manners is simply one more indication to others of the level of your sophistication. If you have excellent table manners, you have conquered a major social hurdle. You'll be a more pleasant and sought-after dinner partner, too, because your poise at the table will make others feel more comfortable and relaxed.

Fortunately, while some other aspects of manners are linked to personal qualities such as tact and the ability to get along with others, table manners can belong to anyone. No one is born with them, and once you have acquired a usable set, it becomes second nature to use them. Another bonus of acquiring good table manners is that learning about them necessitates picking up knowledge about food and wines, and that has become a fascinating avocation for many persons.

The cardinal rules of table manners are to do what is considerate of others and to take the simple approach. Fortunately, the days are long gone when an eagle-eyed dowager rated you socially according to the direction in which you moved your soup spoon. The kind of poor table manners that are really noticed and abhorred are those that offend other's sensibilities—putting used silverware on the table, talking with your mouth full, or waving silverware around, to name only a few of the more common offenses. Of course, there is always the matter of polish— knowing a few deft maneuvers that will show you really know your way around the table. In this chapter, the basics are explained along with a few of the special touches that will serve anyone well at the poshest club in town.

Once you have mastered the essentials of eating properly, it is fine to be somewhat casual about them. Many of the strict and unnecessary rules of even a decade ago have vanished. For example, it is not particularly important to follow the old rule about opening a dinner-sized napkin halfway and a luncheon napkin all the way. Remembering to put the napkin in your lap is the important thing and the only thing you really need to know to avoid being a boor.

SETTING THE TABLE

The first requisite of good table manners is to become familiar with the table settings you are likely to encounter. Particularly in restaurants, meals are served in courses; that is, various foods are brought to the table in a sequence and different plates, flatware, and glassware are used during each course. Even at an informal family dinner, where the meal is not served in courses but is brought to the table all at once, the plates, glasses, and flatware will frequently reflect the tradition of serving food in courses.

At a very formal dinner, the order of courses is as follows: appetizer, soup, fish, meat (usually accompanied by vegetables), salad and cheeses, and dessert. Seven-course dinners are rarely served today, and you are more likely to encounter soup, meat, salad, and dessert or a meal consisting of appetizer, entrée (either meat or fish), and dessert.

The drawing that follows shows the typical plates, flatware, and glasses that one is liable to encounter at an average, not-too-formal meal at home or in a restaurant.

Luncheon or semi-formal dinner

At even the most formal dinner, you will not usually be confronted with more than three forks, and there will rarely be a need for more than two spoons and possibly two knives at the side of the plate (more flatware may be brought in with various courses). An easy rule governs the order in which flatware is used: work in from the outside, that is, start with the first fork or spoon on the outside of the setting and use each consecutive piece of flatware as each course is served.

Glasses

The water goblet should rest at the point of your knife. Except at the most formal of dinners, a large assortment of glasses is not seen. The use of glassware is easy, for someone will fill the glasses, and you have only to drink what is put in them at the appropriate time. The water goblet will be obvious and, in a good restaurant, quickly filled with water. The wine glasses, if there are two, are for red and white wine. They are often the same shape and slightly different sizes. As you drink the wines, try to replace the glasses in approximately the same position at the table, but don't make a fetish of it. It's more important to enjoy what they contain.

Flatware

The smallest fork is for seafood. It may appear to the outside on the fork side or to the outside on the knife side or it may be brought with the seafood course. It is used for eating shrimp cocktails, snails, clams, oysters, or any other seafood appetizer. It is not used when you have ordered fish as an entrée.

The largest fork is for the entrée, be it fish, fowl, or meat. The slightly smaller fork beside the entrée fork is usually meant to be used for the salad. Until fairly recently salads were eaten after the entrée in the United States, as is still the custom in Europe. In the early part of the century in California, where all casual living seems to originate, the custom of serving the salad before the entrée or sometimes even at the very beginning of the meal began to prevail, and most Americans adopted this custom. In the 1970s, as interest in gourmet eating grew, Americans who were knowledgeable about these things once again took to eating the salad after the entrée so it could fulfill its true purpose, which is to cleanse the palate and prepare it for dessert or after-dinner liqueurs. This has caused a small degree of confusion regarding the position of the salad fork. If the salad is to be served before the main course, the salad fork should be placed on the outside between the seafood fork and the entrée fork or to the left of the entrée fork. If the salad is to be served later, the salad fork will be on the inside, or to the right, indicating that the entrée will be eaten first. Sometimes persons who are making the switch to more sophisticated eating bring the salad out later but forget to reposition the fork. Just remember to use the correct fork: the entrée fork, which is the largest one, when the entrée is brought out, the salad fork, which is slightly smaller, when the salad is brought out.

The dinner knife (again, the big one) will be the inside knife to the right of the plate. Next to it will be the beverage spoon, and next to that will be the soup spoon, if soup is to be one of the courses.

Another large spoon that sometimes shows up is the dessert spoon. Optional flatware you may encounter includes a fish or steak knife, which will be to the outside of the dinner knife before the spoons.

Dessert spoons or forks may or may not be at the table when you sit down. If they are present, they will either be on the inside positions next to the plate or they will be at the top of the plate. They can be brought to the table with the dessert plate. If they arrive on the plate, remove them and place them beside the plate to facilitate the serving of dessert; the fork goes on the left and the spoon goes on the right.

Plates

The bread plate, accompanied by the small butter knife, is placed slightly to the left and above the dinner plate.

The salad plate (or bowl, as is often seen today) goes to the left of the dinner plate.

The small extra plate on the dinner plate that is so often seen in restaurants is meant to hold the seafood or appetizer course or the soup. It is a superfluous plate whose only function is to protect the dinner plate until it is used. You don't have to worry about it; the waiter will remove it if it isn't needed, as will a host at a home dinner party.

Finger Bowls

At a very formal dinner you may encounter a finger bowl, which is placed above and to the left of the dinner plate. The finger bowl is not used until you have finished dessert, even though it may be brought to the table with the dessert plate and flatware.

Finger bowls may also appear before the meal at a Chinese or Japanese dinner, in which case they are to be used before the meal. Whether they appear preceding a meal or following a meal, the technique is the same. Dip your fingers into the water and move them to slightly below table level to dry your hands on the napkin.

HANDLING EACH COURSE

Aside from the myriad questions that arise about eating in general, here are a few tips to help you handle each course.

Seafood

Use the small fork and eat on the plate that is put in front of you. Sometimes seafoods come in small casserole platters that the waiter places beside your dinner plate. Use a large spoon to transfer the food from the casserole to the small plate on top of your entrée plate. If necessary, request a large serving spoon to facilitate this process.

Soup

The important rule here is, *Don't slurp*. Actually, any book for adults should not have to make this point but, in fact, it is amazing to see the number of persons who slurp their food or talk while they eat. So be forewarned but not nervous: an occasional sound may be unavoidable and easily handled with a small, murmured apology, but constant slurping—or talking with food in your mouth—is the first sign of a boor.

It is fine to drink from a soup cup with two handles or no handles, but if you feel uncomfortable doing so, it is equally acceptable to use your soup spoon. Formal etiquette books state that the diner should move the spoon away from the body. This is the kind of rule that, fortunately, one no longer need worry about. Just eat the soup quietly, without slurping or spilling it. (Of course, it never hurts to eat exactly correctly; in this case, by moving the spoon away.) Rest the soup spoon in the soup bowl if it is large and flat, or on the plate or saucer under it. If you want to drink the last tasty drop (and who doesn't) but it eludes you, tilt the bowl slightly away from you and spoon it out. Small oyster crackers can be put directly into a bowl of soup, but it is not acceptable to break larger crackers into the soup.

Entrée

Historically speaking, in French menu parlance, entrées were small dishes that accompanied or followed the appetizer and prepared the palate for the *pièce de résistance* that was served later. Today the word "entrée" more often refers to the main dish, although some French cookbooks still make the distinction. An entrée or main dish, which generally consists of meat, fish, or poultry and accompanying vegetable dishes, is eaten with the large fork and knife.

Salad

Generally try to use a salad fork to cut lettuce or other greens. If you meet resistance, using a knife and fork is perfectly correct. The salad plate should be to the left, unless the waiter or host has placed it in the center of the dinner plate, in which case it should be left where it is. When finished, leave the fork on the salad plate.

Fruit

The fruit course increasingly appears with or following salad these days. It sometimes substitutes for dessert, a tribute to the calorie-conscious decade in which we live. At formal American dinners, fruit is peeled, quartered, cut up, and eaten with a fork. It is eaten this way at any type of European dinner. If you are at anything less than a black-tie, five-course formal dinner, however, simply pick up a nice red juicy apple and bite into it. Of course, there are those occasions when one simply feels more elegant peeling and cutting up a piece of fruit, and there is no reason not to do so—just do whatever is most comfortable for you.

Dessert

Dessert may come with a fork or spoon; either will obviously be intended for use with the dessert, so merely eat away, leaving the utensils on your dessert plate when you have finished.

DINING

One can handle one's utensils according to the American or the Continental method or use a combination of both methods. Most Americans, unless they have spent a great deal of time in Europe, are more comfortable with the American method, which is common in the United States. In fact, if you are not comfortable using the Continental method, it will only look awkward, so while you may be tempted to try it, do so only in the privacy of your own home until you are sure you have mastered it. The drawing here shows how to hold the utensils to cut food regardless of whether you will use the American or Continental method to transfer the food to your mouth.

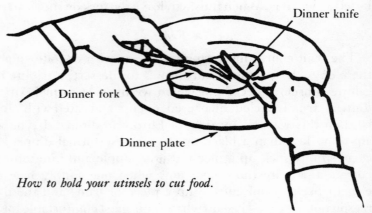

How to hold your utinsels to cut food.

Hold the knife in the right hand with your index finger on the handle slightly overlapping the blade. Hold the fork, prongs down, in your left hand. Elbows should be kept just slightly above the table level.

The American method entails holding the fork in your left hand and the knife in your right hand and cutting the meat, then switching the food on the fork to your right hand before raising it to your mouth. (See the drawing.) Obviously, this method necessitates replacing the knife on the plate before transferring the food to the right hand.

In the Continental style of eating, the food is transferred to the mouth on the fork in the left hand. (See the drawing.)

The American Method.
Lay your knife on the plate, transfer the fork, with the prongs up, to your right hand, and then carry the food to your mouth.

The Continental Method.
With your left hand, bring the fork, prongs down, to your mouth.

Many persons prefer to use the Continental style of eating for everything but the meat, when they switch to the American method. Whatever method you choose to use, try to use it regularly so that you will feel comfortable with it. Some unacceptable ways of holding utensils are shown below.

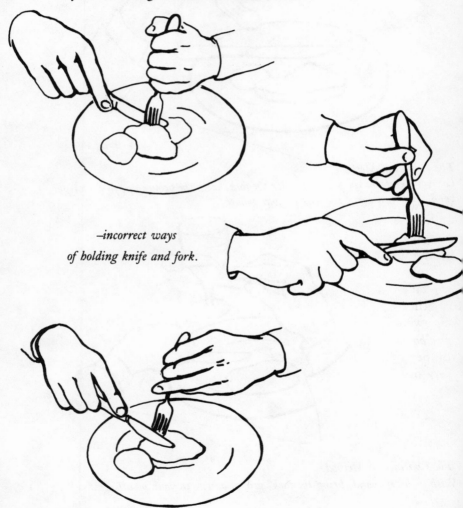

*—incorrect ways
of holding knife and fork.*

When you are finished eating, place your knife and fork together on your plate, as shown in the drawing.

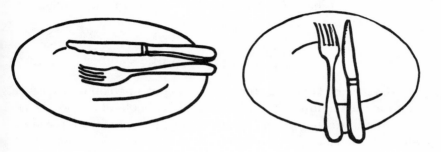

The Finish Position, Continental and American Methods.

SITTING DOWN

Always move to the right of the chair when you are sitting down; this is especially important for women who are being seated by a waiter, for this is what the waiter will expect women to do.

Without being stiff, make an effort to sit erectly at table. Good posture goes hand in hand with self-confidence, and slouching at the table is not a look you will want to present. The old elbows-off-the-table routine has pretty much been boiled down to elbows-off-the-table-while-you-are-eating. It is permissible to put *an elbow* on the table between courses or when you are talking after dinner—or even over coffee, for that matter. Just be careful not to rely on your elbows for support.

EXCUSING YOURSELF

If for any reason you have to leave the table during a meal, excuse yourself to those present; don't just get up and leave.

Reasons for leaving the table include the need to blow your nose, a sudden feeling of illness, and the need to make a trip to the restroom or take a phone call. Leave quietly to avoid making any kind of fuss. When you return, reseat yourself quietly and join in the conversation whenever appropriate.

USING THE NAPKIN

As a general rule, wait for the host to put a napkin in his or her lap and then follow suit, or so the etiquette books of old say. What is important is to put the napkin in your lap shortly after you sit down. The rules for unfolding a napkin have also become more casual: just open it to a comfortable size and put it in place. When you have finished eating, place the napkin casually to your left. Do not refold it.

Use the napkin to remove food crumbs from your lips before you drink a beverage. This avoids leaving a messy wine glass. Lipstick stains on a glass are also unattractive, but it is difficult to tell a woman who looks good in dark red lipstick to wipe it off before she eats. (One trick is to blot it carefully with tissue when it is applied.) Just remember that lipstick on a glass repels some persons—and one of those persons might be your boss.

MAKING CONVERSATION

No one likes a loudmouth, but this distracting feature of a personality can be especially alarming when eating in public. Try always to speak in low, intimate tones at the table. There are some subjects that, even these days, are not acceptable at the table. Details of illness, surgery, funerals, and anything that could make someone squeamish are topics to avoid. Remember that it is considerate to avoid not merely topics that make *you* squeamish, but also whatever might make anyone else uncomfortable.

Although well-mannered people talk freely of money, politics, and religion these days, the table is still not the best place to do so. For one thing, everyone is there to eat, and it is upsetting when one person presses an argument that makes others uncomfortable.

TALKING TO PERSONS WHO SERVE YOU

The days of servants are mostly gone, so you don't have the problem of deciding whether or not to converse with an old family retainer, but some persons do eat regularly in their favorite restaurants and get to know those who help them. Persons who wait on you always deserve a fair measure of respect (especially if you hope for good service), and someone to whom you are friendly when you eat alone should be accorded the same respect when you are with friends. Generally it is polite to thank a waiter occasionally during a meal. You need not thank them for every little service; certainly you do thank someone who performs an extra service.

REACHING

Reaching across the table used to be strictly taboo. Today persons are a little more realistic and generally take whatever is within reach of them, provided they do not have to stretch in front of another person to do so. If something is equidistant from everyone at the table, don't ask someone else to hand it to you but pick it up yourself.

ASKING FOR WHAT YOU NEED

Too many persons are timid, particularly in a restaurant, about asking for something they need or want, or about requesting a change in their food if it is not properly prepared. Since a good executive needs to be aggressive, it only makes sense to apply the same aggression to such a seemingly minor situation as ordering and eating a meal. This is not to say that you should ever be the cause of a scene (a mistake too many would-be stars make), but rather that you should firmly and politely insist on getting what you want or ordered.

DEALING WITH PESTS IN FOOD

Occasionally a water glass or salad will arrive with a small beast in it. The correct way to handle this is not to bring it to the attention of the others present at the table but to quietly request that the waiter remove the offending dish or glass and bring you a fresh one. Use the same technique for unclean flatware or dishes.

REMOVING FOOD FROM YOUR MOUTH

Seeds, pits, and small bones obviously cannot be swallowed, so do the obvious thing and remove them discreetly, placing them on the side of your plate. Use your fingers, cupping them to hide the food, and also bring your napkin to your mouth.

EATING FOOD THAT IS TOO HOT

If you take a bite of food that is too hot to swallow comfortably, squelch it with water—again, as discreetly as can be arranged. Never spit it out.

USING CATSUP AND OTHER SAUCES

Americans, perhaps because they have for a long time lacked the elegant sauces of French cuisine, drench foods in catsup, steak sauce, and anything else that appears on the table in a glass jar. They have even taken to putting catsup on foods such as scrambled eggs. Most etiquette books point out that this is an insult to the chef. Most Americans don't seem to care. If, however, you are dining or lunching with someone you want to impress, it is safer not to drench a good piece of beef or (heaven forbid) your scrambled eggs with anything that was not prepared by the chef. Particularly in light of the reviving interest in gourmet cooking, an increasing number of persons look disdainfully upon such actions.

If you simply cannot eat a food without catsup or another bottled sauce, at least learn to use it correctly. Catsup, mustard, or any other condiment is put directly on an open-faced or closed sandwich. If you want to eat catsup with your French fries, do not drench them in it. Rather, pour a small amount of catsup on the side of the plate and dip the French fries in it as you eat them.

USING JAMS, JELLIES, AND BUTTER

Jams and jellies should be transferred to your serving plate with the spoon that arrives with them; then use your butter knife to spread them on bread or rolls. Pats of butter are transferred with a fork; you may then use your knife to spread it on a roll or your fork to put it on vegetables.

STIRRING AND MASHING FOOD

Even in these days of casual manners, stirring and mashing food have not become acceptable and are, furthermore, highly offensive to others.

USING BREAD TO CLEAN THE PLATE

It is acceptable to use a piece of bread to get at a difficult bit of food; it is less acceptable to use the bread to wipe your plate absolutely clean.

DRINKING

There is an art to drinking beverages when eating food. First, wipe your mouth with your napkin; then sip the beverage. This may sound time-consuming, but it prevents the unattractive situation that results when food particles have traveled far from your mouth across your face, as well as when food particles land on a drinking glass. If you have ever tried to carry on a conversation with someone who has a particle of food located somewhere on his or her face, then you will appreciate the beauty of the required sweep of the lip area with the napkin.

DEALING WITH DROPPED SILVER OR FOOD

Anyone can drop a piece of silver or food. Let's hope common sense can prevail in this situation. If, at the conclusion of the meal, you can quickly and quietly reach for whatever has dropped, do so; if not, leave it.

REMOVING DISHES

Especially when you are eating out with others, do not push your plate away from you, stack your dishes, or even move any dishes. In so doing, you are likely to move the dishes closer to someone you are eating with, and if they are unsightly enough for you to want them out of sight, imagine how they will appear to the other person.

A general rule of thumb in the United States is to serve from the left and remove dishes from the right, and in a fine restaurant, this is how food will be brought to you and taken away. In casual situations, a host or hostess may elect to take the food away from either side. It is never polite to reach across a guest to remove a dish, so as a host you should plan to do whatever is most convenient for the person seated.

DEALING WITH FOOD SPILLED ON THE TABLE

If you break bread or rolls over your bread plate, there will be few crumbs on the tablecloth. If you do drop crumbs on the table, just leave them alone. Small particles of food can be discreetly removed with a napkin when the dishes are cleared or slightly before.

HANDLING USED FLATWARE

Again the rules are only meant to make you easier to eat with, so put used flatware on the plate. Nothing is more glaringly offensive than dirty flatware placed on a white tablecloth, or even on a bare table. Also, remember not to use your flatware to dish up portions of food; wait or ask for serving pieces.

SHARING FOOD

Etiquette books used to advise an elaborate ritual for sharing food in a public place; it involved calling the person who served you and asking his or her assistance. This is no longer recommended. In fact, in some ethnic restaurants, diners are expected to order several dishes and share them; if you plan to do this, explain to the waiter when you order and request any extra plates and flatware that you will need. If something simply looks so delectable that you can't resist sharing when it comes to your table, work out your own arrangements. The best method is to hand a plate, such as the bread plate, across the table to the one who has offered the food. The food is put on the plate and passed back. Far more tricky (and not in particularly good taste) is to pass the food across the table perched precariously on a fork; it is likely to drop off onto the tablecloth.

It is wise to remember to be a bit more reticent about sharing at a business lunch, particularly if you are interviewing for a position or otherwise trying to impress someone; food is not shared as casually under these circumstances as it is among friends.

SMOKING AND NOT SMOKING

Smoking at meals is a touchy subject. It is only civilized to refrain from smoking while anyone at the table is still consuming food, if anyone at the table indicates that he or she has an allergy or is ill, or even if you notice that someone appears to be annoyed by smoke. It is never polite or considerate to smoke during the courses of a formal meal, and if you notice that there are no ash trays on a table in someone's home, take that as a hint that you are expected to refrain at least until after leaving the table.

EATING TRICKY FOODS

There was a time when etiquette books contained detailed accounts of how to eat foods that most American simply were never served. Today, the accounts are more appropriate, because Americans are eating a wider variety of foods, many of which are indeed tricky to handle.

If you are confronted with something you are not sure how to eat, never be afraid to speak up and say, "I've never eaten this before. How do I go about it?" This should never be a cause for embarrassment. Invariably someone at the table will give you instructions and not think another thing about the incident. The paragraphs that follow contain useful descriptions of how to handle certain unusual foods. The only problem is that reading about eating them and eating them are not the same thing. The solution is to cook some of the foods that appeal to you at home and *practice*.

Seafood

SHRIMP COCKTAIL

Use the seafood fork. Eat each shrimp in one bite if the shrimp is small. If it is large, eat it in two bites. Place the fork on the plate under the seafood dish when you are finished.

Oysters and Clams

In open shells, oysters and clams are usually served on a plate of cracked ice. Use a seafood fork. Hold the shell in place with one hand, and with the fork, lift the whole oyster or clam out of the shell and eat it in one bite. Do not pick up the shell. Seafood sauce is usually served in a small bowl placed right in the middle of the ice; dip each piece in it before eating.

Steamed Clams

Use your fingers to lift out each clam by its neck, then pull the body from it and discard the neck part. Dip the clam in melted butter or broth (often served separately) and eat it in one bite. Special note: If a clam shell hasn't opened during the cooking, don't eat it. The closed shell means it shouldn't be eaten.

Snails

Snails are served in shells on a special plate that holds each shell in place. First, pick up and hold a shell with your napkin (snails are always hot) or with the special metal clamps usually served with snails; with the other hand dig out the snail with a seafood fork and eat it in one bite. If you like, you may sip the liquid from the shell, or you may dip small pieces of bread in it with your fork to soak up the butter-and-garlic sauce.

Lobster

If lobsters are not cracked in the kitchen (and you may request this), they are always served with a tool that looks like a nutcracker. Use it to crack the two big claws and then break them wider apart with your hands. Next, pick up one claw and, with the seafood fork, dig out the meat in one or more chunks and put it on your plate. Cut it into bite-sized pieces as you eat it. A butter sauce is served for dipping. Break the small claws with your fingers and either suck out the meat or dig it out with your fork. The coral-colored roe of the lobster and the soft green liver—both considered delicacies—are eaten with a fork.

Meat

CHICKEN

Eat chicken with a knife and fork unless you are at a picnic or a drive-in where no forks are supplied. Steady the piece of chicken on your plate with your fork in one hand. With the other hand cut away the meat a bite at a time.

FROGS' LEGS

Frogs' legs can be eaten partly with a knife and fork, and partly with the fingers. First, though, sever the leg at the joint, then eat as much meat as possible from the larger part, using your knife and fork. Put the bones back on the side of your plate.

SAUCES

Horseradish, applesauce, mint jelly, béarnaise, and cranberry sauce are placed on your dinner plate, either to the side or over the meat. Dip small pieces of food into the sauce one at a time as you eat. Sauces such as lemon-and-butter sauce or tartar sauce are never poured over the whole fish. Instead cut off a small piece of fish and dip it into the sauce.

ARTICHOKES

To begin eating an artichoke, pull off one leaf at a time and dip it into melted butter or sauce. Then pull it through your teeth, scraping off the soft part at the end of the leaf. Set the rest aside. When all the outer leaves are finished and arranged neatly on a side plate, remove the fuzzy part in the middle of the artichoke by cutting under it and lifting it off. Then cut the artichoke heart into pieces and dip each piece into sauce with your fork before eating it.

ASPARAGUS

Eat the soft tips of asparagus with your fork only and then cut the tender part of the stem with a knife and fork, if necessary.

BAKED POTATOES

Do not scoop baked potatoes onto your plate and mash them; instead, eat them out of the potato shell. Use the dinner fork to put butter on the potato. You may cut up the skin with a dinner knife and fork and eat it.

FRENCH FRIED POTATOES

Eat fried potatoes with a fork after cutting them into shorter lengths, if necessary. Never spear a piece and bite away at it from your fork. At a drive-in or on a picnic, French fries become finger food.

Fruits

BANANAS

When served whole at the table, bananas should be peeled halfway or all the way and the skin put aside on your plate. Then the banana is eaten by breaking off pieces with your fingers or by cutting them off with a knife and fork. Do not chomp away at a half-peeled banana with the skin draped down over your hand.

TANGERINES

Peel tangerines; then eat one segment at a time, preferably in two bites. Use the fingers.

ORANGES

Peel oranges spirally if you can do it gracefully. Then eat them segment by segment with the fingers.

GRAPES

Cut or break grapes from the main bunch in small clusters, put them on your dessert plate, and eat them from there one by one. Do not pick one grape at a time from the main dish. Remove seeds from your mouth with your fingers and put them on the side of your plate.

STRAWBERRIES

Strawberries can be picked up by the hulls and dipped in whatever is served with them—sugar, whipped cream, or sour cream—and eaten with the fingers. Fruit in juice is always eaten with a spoon.

LEMON

A slice of lemon served on meat or fish is not picked up; it is strictly for show. A wedge of lemon is picked up and squeezed or pressed against the prongs of a fork to let the juice trickle out. Shelter it with your hand to avoid spraying anyone.

Miscellaneous

OLIVES

Olives belong on the butter or salad plate, but if neither is provided, put them on a dinner plate. If an olive is large and has a pit, eat it with two or three bites, holding it with your fingers. Place the pit on the butter or salad plate. Small olives without pits can be eaten whole, but be careful not to consume them at the same rate you would eat popcorn or peanuts.

SPAGHETTI

There are three ways of eating spaghetti. (1) Cut a few of the strands and wind them around the tines of the fork until you form a small ball. (2) Hold the fork in the right hand and the spoon in your left. Pick up spaghetti with the tines of the fork and turn it around against the bowl of the spoon, continuing to roll until no ends are hanging. If ends do dangle, bite the ends off before you put the rolled ball into your mouth. Never suck up the ends at the end. (3) Proceed as in (2) but use just the fork, winding a few strands around the tines of the fork with the aid of the spoon.

CANDY OR PASTRY IN PAPER FRILLS

Pick up pastry or candy paper and all when you are served. Put both food and paper on the tablecloth beside your plate until you are ready to eat it, then pick up just the food and eat it. For dessert, use your fork to ease the food off the paper before eating it.

TOOTHPICKS

Never use toothpicks in public.

CHAPTER 9

Business Travel
and Conventions

WHETHER YOU ARE GOING to an annual convention or traveling abroad as a representative of your company for the first
time, a special etiquette surrounds business travel, and it helps to
know how to play the game before you get there. In addition,
there is often too little variation in the kinds of entertaining that
occur at conventions, so this chapter contains some innovative
ideas for impressing important clients when entertaining them in
strange cities.

AIRPLANE ETIQUETTE

Most business travel today is done by airplane. For years airlines have promoted the friendliness of their employees, and
frankly, it is about time the rest of the world reciprocated. All the
airlines we interviewed, however, did report that their smoothest,
most courteous travelers were those who traveled regularly on
business.

Reservations

Have your secretary or assistant make airline reservations and any other travel arrangements as soon as you have set a firm date for the trip. Tickets—and sometimes even boarding passes—can be picked up far in advance to cut down on the amount of time you have to spend waiting in airports.

When Things Go Wrong

Not only are things more likely to go wrong when you are traveling, but many persons find themselves falling apart over what would be only minor issues at home. It helps to stay calm. It helps even more to be courteous. The airline cannot help it if you are snowbound in an airport or city where you do not want to be snowbound. Remember, too, that airline personnel also suffer when passengers cannot get to their planned destinations; they are deluged by miserable people. Therefore, it only makes sense that they will dispense courtesies such as alternative transportation, free food, and lodging more freely to those persons who have made an impression on them, and courtesy makes a far better impression than outrage does. The best strategy is to be persistent but polite. Make it clear that you want to get out on the first available airplane, but be courteous and even chatty when telling airline personnel of your needs.

When a Complaint Is Called For

Sometimes service is too surly to ignore or you have truly been done an injustice. When you must make a complaint while traveling, firmness and courtesy will help you to do so faster, and speed is usually the essential element of business travel. One executive was rushing to catch a plane when a security person managed to turn her purse upside down, causing her keys, a good pen, and a business notebook to go flying in all directions. No one made the slightest effort to help her retrieve her things. After she had to move at fast trot to try to catch her plane, her anger grew, despite the fact that security was separate from the airline and therefore of no real consequence to the person she would be dealing with at the check-in counter. Still, lacking any other immediate source to complain to, she decided to explain what had made her angry in the hope that the airplane employee would pass on the complaint.

She managed to complain with grace and tact, saying, "I know this isn't your fault, but I was just treated rudely and in a way that could have caused me to miss this plane at security. I would like to complain to security directly, but I am sure the airline would also like to know that their passengers are being treated carelessly. Would you please pass this on to your boss or someone who can talk directly to the head of security?"

Since the person to whom you make a complaint about poor service is rarely the one who mistreated you (always ask to talk to the boss, if possible), the words, "I know this isn't your fault," can go a long way to ease the pain of a coming complaint.

On the Plane

Airline personnel, including flight attendants, are highly trained professionals and deserve to be treated with respect and courtesy. While a variety of special services are available, such as blankets, hot tea or coffee, aspirin or other medication, and magazines, these are extra services, so phrase any requests for them as politely as possible, and be sure to thank the person who helps you.

Flight attendants may have time to sit down and chat with the passengers, but this is not, in fact, part of their jobs, so don't expect it.

En Route

Many business persons plan to work while en route, which poses no problem unless the person next to you wants to chat. If opening a briefcase and spreading papers out over the tray in front of your seat is not enough to discourage chatter, a more direct approach is called for. It is quite polite to say, "I would like to talk to you, but I am afraid I have to get this work done." Even if you are reading a book for pleasure (half the world views this as being occupied and the other half seems to consider it doing nothing), you can say, "I'm sorry I can't talk right now, but I'm very absorbed in this book."

If the flight is short and you do plan to work, probably the best place to do it is in a window seat. On long trips, however, most experienced travelers prefer aisle seats for the easy access they provide to all parts of the plane. When you must cross someone's seat to leave yours, say "Excuse me" when leaving and when returning. Rather than inconveniencing others sharing the row of seats, request any special services from the flight attendants.

Requests for special diets required for health or religious reasons are gladly met by the airlines, but you need to mention your needs when buying your ticket so the food can be ordered and placed on the plane. Nonpork meals, kosher meals, and special dietary plates are not automatically available to those who do not request them in advance, but almost any special diet will be prepared at no extra cost for a passenger.

Deplaning

Since the flight attendants are the persons who have hosted your trip and made it as pleasant as they could, there is one often overlooked courtesy that attendants truly appreciate: the passenger who says "Thank you" when deplaning.

If a flight has been delayed en route and you are late for an important meeting, it is helpful to explain quietly your need to deplane immediately to an attendant who will then make sure you are one of the first persons off the plane.

EXPENSE ACCOUNT ETIQUETTE

This book will not present a lesson about fudging on your expense account. If you decide to do that, you're on your own. In some companies, some areas of expense accounts are left very open, but this is a matter of company policy, and there is no etiquette involved other than to check discreetly with others to see what is and is not possible.

It is assumed that business entertaining is done on an expense account, particularly when one is out of town at a convention or traveling in a foreign country. Rarely will a customer or client even offer to pay the tab. These things are simply taken for granted by persons who are used to them, so if a business colleague asks you to join him or her under these circumstances, accept your guest status graciously.

On the other hand, when you are using an expense account to entertain someone, it is best to be discreet about it. A potential or present customer or client with any business sophistication will not be impressed by your ability to spend the company's money freely and may well be offended.

Occasionally a client, if given the opportunity, will suggest an expensive restaurant that you feel is out of line for the occasion or your expense account. One way to avoid this is to suggest a restaurant when asking someone to lunch or dinner. If you have forgotten to do this, however, and a client has grabbed the chance for a splendid freebie, you still can steer things a little more in the direction you would like them to go. Simply say: "Oh, I was thinking of eating at Jake's Steak House—it's quieter there, and I thought we would have more of a chance to talk." If the client insists on the fanciest restaurant in town, you are, of course, stuck, but it is a rare person who will have the nerve to do so.

If you are trying to opt for less lavish entertaining, never blame it on your company—this makes you look disloyal and it makes the company look cheap, neither of which is good for your image.

CONVENTIONS

Aside from the travel that may be a routine part of a job, conventions are the other occasion when an executive may be called upon to represent a company. There is no denying the freer atmosphere that generally prevails at conventions—many persons view conventions as one big party—and you will indeed want to participate in some of the festivities, yet a smart executive never forgets that the real purpose of a convention is work, namely, representing the company. Whether you are doing direct selling, making new contacts, presenting a new product line, or entertaining major clients, the main purpose is business, not socializing.

If you are in charge of setting up a corporate display or doing the entertaining for a convention, let the previous year's budget serve as a guideline of what to spend this year. If files are available, it is also a good idea to go over them to see what has been done in the past.

Entertaining Important Clients

Most of the routine matters of convention work, such as setting up and operating a display booth, will not be handled by executive personnel, but the entertaining of important clients is usually too important a task to leave to anyone else. Draw up lists of persons you want to entertain.

If you are planning a big bash, make arrangements well in advance, since every other company at the convention will have the same idea. Food and service arrangements for parties to be held at a hotel are always made by the hotel. Functions outside a hotel, however, can be handled by a caterer, and this is where some truly innovative entertaining ideas can be put to work. Call the local tourist's bureau and ask them to recommend interesting local or historic sites that might be attractive places in which to entertain guests. Find out whom to contact and how to go about making arrangements. Many towns have lovely small museums where small private dinners can be held; historical homes or other sites can often be rented, particularly if a company is willing to throw in a donation. Is there an outdoor concert center where you might invite people for dinner and a concert? Is the city's local opera or symphony group an outstanding attraction? Is there an ex-president's home or the home of some other famous person that might be available for a function? In a city with a river or an attractive lakefront, a yacht or riverboat party quickly comes to mind.

The hardest-working persons at conventions often spend the entire stay in the hotel headquarters or the convention center, so they frequently welcome the opportunity to relax away from the hotel and see something of the place they are visiting—and it is an added bonus if the event is combined with seeing business associates. Too many companies resort to the monotonous cocktail-party-in-the-suite routine, so if you really want to impress a few top clients, try to find something interesting and of local interest to entertain them. Go for an elegant dinner; the persons you are entertaining may have been subsisting for several days on hotel food caught on the run.

Invitations to such functions need to be extended well in advance of the convention. Either call or write an important client or customer to confirm the date; competition for people's time is never more fierce than at a convention, so put in your bid early.

Throwing a Big Bash

If you decide to give one big bash—it may be a tradition and it certainly is a good way to entertain a large group—planning must be done well in advance. Talk to a hotel party planner or a caterer's representative. Find out exactly what services and what food can be offered, what kind of bar can be set up, how the food will be served, and what the quality and grade of the food will be, as well as what security arrangements can be made, if necessary.

Party crashers are a real problem at conventions, but when you are spending your company's money to entertain clients, you have a right to control who attends even the largest party. Equally important is to be on the alert for someone obnoxious enough to ruin the spirit of the party. Conventioneers who are making the rounds of several parties don't get any mellower as the evening wears on, so either you or someone you have appointed or hired should be authorized to remove unauthorized guests. (An unauthorized guest is someone who does not know the name of your company or the nature of its business or who cannot name a single employee.) Such persons should be politely but firmly asked to leave. Never permit anyone to make a scene over removing someone from the room; however public the occasion or large the party, it is still a business function and it is better to let a pest or uninvited person stay than to use bouncer's tactics to get rid of him or her, a quick damper to any party.

The same general rules of good taste that apply to entertaining clients at lunch or elsewhere in your own community apply at conventions. Representatives of the company do not eat as if they were being served their last meal. They should assume the role of host, circulating among the guests and subtly (or not so subtly, depending upon the occasion) conducting business.

INTERNATIONAL TRAVEL

In these days of multinational corporations, executives are frequently asked to represent their companies abroad or even to live in another country for several years. International travel—particularly for large companies—has become rather commonplace, whereas it used to be a plum that went only to company presidents and top executives.

Even if you are planning a personal trip to another country, sometimes it is possible to work this into a work assignment—so it certainly is worthwhile to announce your travel plans at work. If you work for a small- to medium-sized company that has one or more clients or suppliers in the place you plan to visit, mention this to your boss and say you would be willing to handle any business that might come up while you're there. If you work for a very large corporation, it will probably own affiliates, branches, or even companies where you are planning to visit. Ask whether you can make arrangements to visit these facilities. Even if your visit is not official company business, any contacts you develop will pay benefits in the long run.

If, on the other hand, the day arrives when your boss calls you into his or her office and asks whether you would be available to go to Germany or Belgium next month, say yes. If this will be your first trip outside the United States, there is no need to announce it openly, although it is certainly nothing to be kept as a dark secret. The reason you should not announce your lack of travel experience is that it might give your superiors second thoughts; travel is an anxiety-producing situation for most persons, and your boss might prefer to send someone who has more travel experience. In fact, if you go to work for a company where there is any possibility of travel outside the United States, get a passport. Then when you are asked to go somewhere, before the question of your travel experience even arises, you can say, "Fine, my passport is up to date. Do you think we can arrange for a visa by next month?"

When you are asked to travel in another country for the company, it is safe to assume that the company will make the arrangements for transportation, accommodations, and any business. Should your secretary fall heir to this assignment, have him or her contact a travel agency with whom your company has done business or any reputable travel agency or the airline you will fly. Airlines will make hotel reservations and reserve a car for you, in addition to booking the flight. As with all business travel, assume that you will fly whatever class you would normally fly for domestic travel for business purposes—increasingly today, that is tourist class. An international trip is definitely not the time to splurge on a first-class ticket, since it is considerably more expensive than domestic first-class. You or whoever is making the travel arrangements should also contact the nearest embassy or consulate of the country you plan to visit; personnel there will be able to answer any specific questions regarding the business you wish to conduct and may even supply you with background reading materials on business and economic conditions in their country.

Travel Documents

Some things you will need to take care of personally. First, you must obtain a passport if you do not have one. Call or visit the nearest passport office. You will have to fill out several forms requesting information such as your parents' birth dates, maiden names of women in your family, and so on, so go prepared with some degree of family history in mind or written down.

It normally takes two to four weeks during nonrush season (fall and winter) to obtain a passport. If your business is pressing, you can make special arrangements to obtain a passport sooner. If you know you are going to need this special service, make it easy on yourself and be very polite to the person who helps you from the first second that you step up to the counter.

To apply for a passport, you will need proof of citizenship (a birth certificate or naturalization papers) and identification that includes your signature and a description or photograph of you. You are required to have passport photos when your application is made. You will need 2- by 2-inch square black-and-white or color photos—there are other restrictions, so try to find someone who specializes in taking passport photos. This is easy in a large city, for the offices of such photographers are always located near the passport agency and the photos can usually be made in one or two hours. In a small community you may have to call several photographers to find someone. A passport costs $13; it can be paid for with a check or money order.

Health certificates and smallpox vaccinations are no longer required by the United States, but other countries sometimes impose restrictions when there is an outbreak of a dangerous disease. As a precaution, about ten days before leaving, call the local health department to check on any inoculations that might be required in the countries where you plan to travel.

Foreign Customs

If you have time, you may want to study the language of the country you plan to visit; for any business trip you will surely need to brush up on the customs. In Europe, persons shake hands more frequently than they do in the United States, so you will want to prepare for this and any other customs (such as whether or not to smoke during a meal) that may present problems. As another example, in Europe, when you are invited to dinner, it is customary to take a small bouquet to the hosts. On the other hand, in some countries certain flowers are not welcome because of local superstition or because they are sent only to funerals—this is the kind of thing you will want to know in advance.

It is flattering to your hosts to have a working knowledge of current news and economics—and, of course, the business you will discuss. No one expects or wants you to be an expert on a strange country, but if a major election has just been held or business has taken a downswing, it shows interest to have advance knowledge of such affairs.

As when conducting any business travel, you will want to stay within the general budgetary practices of your company, but the guidelines are generally a little more lax in foreign countries. Many executives, for example, rent limousines for local travel. It saves them time and it impresses people with their corporate status.

If you want to do any entertaining, ask the advice of local persons and then follow it. Do not expect to be invited to the homes of those you see during the day; this is done less frequently in foreign countries than in the United States. If you want to see a business associate for dinner (either to work or to repay courtesy shown to you), ask him or her to be your guest at a restaurant and then suggest one that you have heard is good. It is courteous to ask if the spouse would like to join you, but do not be surprised if this invitation is declined. A sharper line is drawn between business and social relationships in other countries—and, of course, in some Middle Eastern and Oriental countries, women are still not included in business of any kind.

Security has increasingly become a problem for high-level corporate executives traveling outside the United States. If your company has security officers, you may want to check with them about any special arrangements. It also helps to have a set routine and to stick to it, so that persons who are depending upon you to show up somewhere will become concerned if you do not. Common courtesy can also be put to work on this front; befriend hotel and restaurant personnel and tell them, for example, whether you will be away for a few days or whether you are planning to return the same evening.

As far as using good manners in a place where they may vary entirely from American standards, while it is courteous to partake of any local customs you are comfortable with, remember that the ways of showing consideration for others do not vary much from culture to culture. The manners you use at home should get you through in a pinch, if they are well-intended. If the style of eating is slightly different, your hosts will probably be ready to take this into account just as you would make exceptions for them were they visiting the United States.

While business associates in the United States may carefully avoid any controversial topics, your hosts in a foreign country may be too curious to do so, or there simply may be no taboos in their culture against discussing political systems, race relations, or any other subject over a social dinner. Capitalism versus socialism or Eurocommunism is a popular topic. If you like, be prepared to discuss and defend your beliefs, but maintain a note of congeniality. Your hosts are more interested in hearing details of a political or social system than they are in being converted to its ways.

There are several places you can go to learn about foreign customs and ways of living. Begin with the consulate or embassy of the country you are planning to visit. Embassies are located in

Washington, D.C., and can be reached in writing or by phone. Consulates, located in other large cities such as Chicago and New York, will also be happy to supply you with any information about local customs or business practices.

You can also check your library or bookstore for books on the country you plan to visit.

If you are planning an extended visit abroad or will be living in another country for any length of time, you may want to contact persons who have lived there. Call your local university to ask if a faculty member has lived in the country of your interest or inquire about local clubs related to the country in which you are interested.

CHAPTER 10

Dressing for Business:
Men

E VER SINCE THE DAY Adam felt he needed to clothe himself
in a fig leaf, clothing has been an important status symbol. It
denotes class and it reveals quite a lot about the money and power
one possesses. Dressing is the way eccentrics give vent to their
need for individuality. It is also a way of showing that one belongs, that one fits in, and that one plays well with the rest of the
team.

The problem, then, with putting on a suit every morning is that
there are many other subleties that must be mastered to make that
suit say what you want it to say about the kind of person you are:
mobile, intelligent, right for your profession.

DECIPHERING UNWRITTEN DRESS CODES:
HOW TO READ THE SIGNALS

Dressing, like so many other areas of good manners, is not
something anyone will necessarily tell you about—if you aren't
doing it right, that is. In fact, by the time you hear that your dress
is inappropriate, permanent damage may well have been done to

197

your career. For example, if a superior calls you in to tell you that full-face beards or any kind of facial hair are not welcomed by your company, he or she has probably been seething about it for several months, and unless you are prepared to shave off that beard immediately in a gesture of deference and then toe the line very carefully, it is safe to assume that some tarnish has been added to your image—with that company anyway.

Of the executives in large corporations, banks, law firms, and middle-sized businesses who were interviewed for this book, none admitted to having a written dress code for their executives. When we wondered about the fact that so many bright young executives had obviously figured out how to dress, largely because of the great similarity in their appearances, one executive laughed and commented: "Why should we have a dress code? The rules are all right there in unwritten form. Those who dress to fit in get ahead. Those who don't—well, they get lost along the way, unless they're too damned brilliant to let that happen to them."

But "fitting in" doesn't necessarily mean dressing in a white shirt and a conservative three-piece suit. The key to successful —and tasteful—dressing lies in observing the successful people in your profession (and your boss is most likely one of those people) and modeling your dress after theirs. You may not be able to afford the same quality of materials as they wear, but the styling should be similar.

For those who bristle at the notion that what they put on their backs is nearly as important as what is in their heads, cheer up. As one company president noted, "Society's much looser now, thank God. I have a mustache now, but when I sold computers for four and a half years, I never wore anything but a white shirt, conservative suit, and a very short haircut. And in four and a half years, I reached the senior executive management level by playing that game, which was more important to me than having a mustache simply because it was in vogue. How you dress depends upon the value judgments you make for yourself. An individual must look the part he or she chooses to play. Then, too, in many businesses, things have eased up considerably, although anyone who wants to get ahead should think long and hard about whether or not he fits the image of the company he works for—whether or not his appearance would irk the most conservative board member." The important thing to remember is to dress to suit those figures of authority who ultimately will control your professional destiny—if you're planning to climb to the top, that is.

BUYING A BUSINESS SUIT

The first consideration in buying a business suit is quality. Buy the best quality you can afford. On the other hand, no one in business should overdress—a $20,000-a-year employee who strolls in wearing a different custom-made $500 suit every morning is immediately suspected of being frivolous at least, and at worst, of having his hand in the till.

Business suits come in three kinds: off the rack, semicustom, and custom. The difference, aside from price, is the amount of special alterations one receives. With an off-the-rack suit, the store will offer you a first fitting, and you will do well to insist on a second fitting when you return to make sure everything has been done according to your specifications. Good stores never charge for alterations on off-the-rack suits, and this alone is worth the extra $50 to $75 you will pay for such suits.

With a semicustom suit, you can choose from among a selection of fabric swatches and a variety of styles and tailoring details. Buying this kind of suit, which costs from $250 to $500, entails several fittings, which are necessary for a man who is hard to fit.

A custom suit costs $500 and up. You can have any fabric and any tailoring detail or style you wish, and if you are in this price range, your tailor or salesman should be telling you what to wear to look well dressed.

Fitting the Suit

Regardless of the kind of suit you buy, you need to know a little about how it should fit. First, consider the fit of the jacket— something that not enough men do. The jacket should fit the back securely; the collar should not stand out at all from the shirt collar, and it should not wrinkle, either vertically or horizontally, across the back when you are standing normally.

Move around in a jacket; it should feel comfortable and should not gap or wrinkle anywhere. Make sure the vents hang properly. Vents on a jacket ensure ease of movement. Generally, two vents are considered sportier and more high fashion, but they also allow greater freedom of movement. A single vent is more traditional, and many older, conservative men have clung to it, despite changing styles. A ventless jacket looks very European—and also looks good only on a slim body in a meticulously fitted suit.

Take a good look at the sleeve of the suit before you buy it. Setting in sleeves is one of the hardest tasks of tailoring and is sometimes poorly done on cheaper suits. Look to see that they are smoothly sewn in. You should be able to move your arm freely without causing the jacket to hike up. The correct, best length of a jacket depends upon your body proportions, but it should be long enough to rest in your bent fingers when they are cupped around the bottom of the jacket when you are standing normally. The sleeve should come to about midway through the wristbone— enough to allow for a half-inch of shirt cuff to show when your arms are hanging at your sides.

A vest requires fitting, too. It should fit smoothly with no wrinkles or gaps, especially at the armholes. For the most success- ful fitting of a suit jacket and vest, wear the same style and weight of shirt that you plan to wear with the suit when you are shopping.

Pants should not be tight; they should fall straight when you are standing and should not bag anywhere. They should have loops for a belt if you are buying a traditional, fairly conservative business suit.

Cuffed pants come and go with the current fashion, although cuffs always continue to be around for sports wear. Cuffs should be about 2 inches deep and worn only on lightweight business suits to avoid the appearance of bulk.

If you have cuffs, have the pants length finished straight across. Their length is best when they break slightly (but only slightly) over the tops of your shoes. A major fault in fitting suits is to make the pants too short, so have them done ½ to ¼ inch longer than you think you need. Uncuffed pants should also break over the tops of your shoes. In the back, they should drop to the tops of the heel of your shoes. Needless to say, you should be wearing the shoes you plan to wear with the suit when it is fitted.

Following Fashion or Fad

Most business suits are strictly tailored. Avoid extra flaps, colored stitching, self-belts, patches or contrasting fabric anywhere, yokes, and anything that is part of the leisure suit look. Designer suits, while beautifully cut and frequently better fitted than other suits, are not really part of the traditional business look. They look effete to many older conservative businessmen, who have yet to accept the fact that men's styles do change, but if you work in a profession where high fashion is accepted or even expected, designer suits may well be the norm.

Watch styles carefully and avoid new ones until they start to show up in the more conservative stores. Single- or double-breasted suits look dated if they are not the current look, as do lapels that are too wide or too narrow, uncuffed pants when cuffs are in fashion, and loosely fitted suits when slightly more fitted ones are in style.

Colors and Fabrics

The best colors for business suits are gray, beige, blue, and shades of these color families. Also acceptable are pin stripes, chalk stripes, and muted plaids. Avoid bright colors (especially in the blue family), pin stripes in garish colors such as rust and scarlet, and any plaid that is not muted.

Men's suits today come in a wide variety of fabrics. Natural fabrics are favored—wool, preferably, or cotton or linen for summer. Some very finely made polyesters look and feel just like wool; if you truly cannot tell them from the real thing, by all means go ahead and buy them. Their great advantage is that they are practically wrinkleproof.

Taking Care of the Suit

The number of times a suit can be worn before it needs pressing varies with the individual and the fabric. It goes without saying, though, that a wrinkled suit looks messy and should be sent off for pressing if not for cleaning.

BUYING SHIRTS

The well-dressed man has learned the secret of buying shirts to go with suits rather than buying the other way around, or worse still, simply collecting shirts and ties. A general guideline is to have three to four shirts for each suit if you have three to five suits, and if you have five to ten or more suits, you can make do with fewer shirts for each suit. Since a shirt is worn only once before laundering, the need for any one color may vary depending on how quickly your laundry can turn around your shirts.

Shirts to go with the basic conservative business suit should be, of course, fairly conservative. This generally means that white, pastels, and pin stripes are most acceptable. Avoid shirts darker than a suit and try to select a tie that is darker than the shirt, or you may find yourself looking like an underworld figure. Shirts should be of dull-finish, flat weaves. Cotton is best, although some men can wear magnificently tailored silk shirts. Shiny fabrics, prints, plaids, wide stripes, and bright colors are out, except for those who work in professions where high fashion is accepted (see "Dressing for Your Profession"). If you opt for striped shirts, those made of white fabric with stripes in subtle colors are preferable. All shirts to be worn under suits should have long sleeves.

Custom-made shirts are expensive, but they are a smaller luxury than a custom-made suit—and they do have status. Custom-made shirts always fit better than ready-mades. Custom shirts do not have pockets, presumably because persons who can afford custom-made shirts need not carry such mundane items as pens and pencils. Very small and very large men also may find it to their advantage to order custom-made shirts for a better fit. In large cities, some stores have semicustom-made shirts, which are just like semicustom-made suits. A variety of fabrics and styles are offered and the shirts are made to your measurements. These shirts sometimes start as low as $25 but can go much higher; sometimes a minimum quantity must be ordered.

BUYING TIES

When you buy shirts to go with a new suit, also plan to buy coordinating ties. The first thing to look for in a tie is fit: it should come to the tip of your belt. Most ties are 55 to 56 inches long. Choose a tie you already own that fits perfectly and use that as a guide when shopping. The more expensive a tie is, the longer it is likely to be, so very short men may find it necessary to order custom-made ties. A tie should have a tab on the back through which the smaller section passes.

Silk is the best tie material, but silk and polyester is a good combination. Again, the best rule of thumb is to buy nothing that looks synthetic, but to go ahead and buy any synthetic that looks and feels real. Wool challis is another good tie material, and cotton ties are often worn in warm climates. The material must be thin enough to hold a neat knot.

Plan to buy a combination of printed and solid ties and also some seasonal ones. In most professions, print ties are acceptable.

The smaller the print, the more acceptable the tie. Polka dots and diagonals are perennial favorites. Club ties and ties that display heraldic emblems, golf balls, fishing gear, and other such tiny prints are acceptable in most corporations, law firms, banks, and businesses, but in sales they may not be, depending upon who your customers are. The same is true for Ivy League ties—some Midwesterners and Westerners see them as signs of the Eastern establishment and just don't like them. The best basic all-round tie is a muted paisley.

For most business purposes, a bow tie is considered too eccentric, although they are still popular among scholars, some lawyers, and others who have risen high enough to wear anything they please.

BUYING ACCESSORIES

When executives were asked what they did to prepare for an important event, such as a meeting with a client or a presentation, they all replied that they got haircuts and had their shoes shined. And while any well-dressed man should know enough to keep his shoes shined and well-heeled, many are at a loss as to the best kinds of shoes to wear for business.

Shoes

Black and brown are the best shoe colors, and laced or wing-tip shoes are worn by most conservative businessmen, although a general loosening in shoe styles has become apparent over the last few years. Plain slip-on shoes are fine as long as they aren't decorated with flashy hardware. Gucci shoes, the status symbol to end all status symbols in men's shoes in New York and Chicago, may not impress conservative Midwesterners.

The emphasis on conservatism may rankle some—particularly those young executives who know they look good in some of the new cuts of men's clothes. This is understandable, but it is helpful to keep in mind that most bosses are older and more conservative. Furthermore, while dress for men has become considerably more interesting in recent years in terms of variety in styles and fabrics, this revolution has mostly taken place in the large cities such as New York, Chicago, and San Francisco. In the rest of the country, the boss who must be impressed with one's ability to dress to fit the corporate image is still conservative and a bit old-school.

Jewelry

Jewelry may be fine for disco dancing on Saturday night, but it does not fit in with the corporate image. Again, it is a matter of pleasing your boss or chairperson of the board, who may be fifty or older and is keeping an eye on you. A wedding band, possibly a small gold ring, and a plain watch are the only acceptable jewelry as far as most corporate business, bank, and law firm executives are concerned. Small gold or silver cuff links are fine, too.

Avoid any symbols that give away your personal life: class rings, which have never had any status, Masonic rings or insignia, religious symbols, and school or regional ties. Anything reminiscent of your school days, as a matter of fact, lacks status and makes a man look immature.

Judging from the number of fancy watches seen today, one would think they are power symbols, yet where it counts—in the board room and the president's office—they aren't. The only real status symbol is a very expensive, plain, thin gold watch. Since most young executives cannot afford this kind of watch, buy a plain serviceable watch with a gold or leather band—the kind that looks more expensive than it is. Of course, if you can lay out the cash for a good-name watch from a jeweler such as Tiffany or Cartier, by all means do so. What even the best class ring won't get you in status, a good label on a watch will.

Handkerchiefs

White handkerchiefs tucked in the front pocket are still seen in many conservative business suits on older men. They look a bit stuffy on young men; on the other hand, most successful, older men reported a distaste for the bright-colored ornamental scarves that are so frequently worn today.

Leather Goods and Umbrellas

Successful dressing calls for paying attention to accessories, too. For example, umbrellas of powerful, successful men are invariably black. A small good leather wallet, or better yet, a pocket secretary that slips in and out of the breast pocket, is a sign of a successful man. Briefcases, particularly for men, should be of the best leather you can afford and preferably brown. A small canvas bag is fine for carrying postwork sports equipment.

Hats

Ironically, there seems to be no hard-and-fast rule about hat styles, even though every man interviewed had his own idea of what he wouldn't be caught dead wearing. To be safe, stick to a plain gray or beige felt hat. To be warm, try one of the fur hats that are popular if not overly stylish. To be noticed—in a way that may or may not please you—you can wear anything from a beret to a Greek fisherman's hat. Some executives even adopt unusual hats as their one departure from totally conservative dress.

Gloves

Gloves are no longer required as a sign of good manners. They are, however, a necessity in a large part of the country during the winter. The glove that works best is leather and brown or dark gray, whatever looks best with your overcoat.

Coats

Coats have a lot of status. If you have money, you can afford to get your coat cleaned often, and that means you can and should wear a beige trench coat. Fairly plain beige trench coats are a true mark of a successful businessman. More leeway is permitted in overcoats; cloth, suede, and leather are fine. Cashmere is the ultimate status symbol for conservative businessmen, and fur coats have won a lot of popularity in cold climates in recent years. They will probably continue to become more acceptable for men, so if you live in a cold climate and you have accepted all the advice given so far about dressing conservatively but you still want to own one outlandish piece of clothing, this is the purchase to consider.

GROOMING

Needless to say, any well-dressed man falls far short of the mark if his personal grooming standards are not as impeccable as his taste in clothing. Deodorants and antiperspirants (most come in combined forms) are a necessity; colognes and scented aftershave, popular a few years ago, are now considered slightly sophomoric.

CHOOSING A HAIR STYLE

Facial hair, a symbol of antiestablishment freedom, is still frowned upon in many places, especially corporations, law firms, and banks. This is a shame because a little well-placed facial hair has been known to hide a wide assortment of defects, such as a receding chin, lips that are too thin, and youthfulness. Some young men continue to go against the mainstream on the subject of facial hair, which, as many executives interviewed for this book repeatedly noted, often calls for a comment from the boss. Unfortunately, by the time the boss comments, he or she is usually pretty steamed about the hair, and the damage to your image may be irreparable. Goatees are definitely unacceptable, possibly because they look too satanic, and handlebar mustaches are thought to indicate a fairly large ego, to say nothing of looking just a little silly on a grown man. Even the executives interviewed who didn't know what handlebar mustaches were called knew they did not like them on their young executives. Full-face beards—a stage that almost no one in a corporation ever gets to anyway—are mostly out of style these days.

DRESSING FOR YOUR PROFESSION

Each profession has an unwritten dress code. A good way to observe the varying codes is to visit a large bank in a big city and ride the elevator with a group of executives, all of whom will be dressed surprisingly alike. Move on to a federal court building and observe the dress of successful lawyers. Persons in publishing and advertising, doctors, and salespeople all seem to have their sets of unwritten rules about dress. The most successful salesmen, several surveys have shown, are invariably those who are best dressed *and* those who dress most like their customers, so salespeople, take note.

Interviews with persons in various professions indicated that there is a lot more room for individual tastes than one might expect. No one gets fired for owning one high-fashion suit or wearing bright ties or even a bow tie occasionally. Very powerful men even use their dress as a power symbol. One executive, who numbers among his acquaintances many chairpersons of the board and company presidents, told of a very successful businessman who always wore a ten-gallon hat while he worked. He wore the hat inside as well as outside his office—a gesture that was both eye-catching and a definite sign that he was the most powerful person in the room.

If you feel the need to be eccentric—and who doesn't occasionally?—go ahead. Just do it politely, which means don't use eccentricity as a power tool, the way the man in the ten-gallon hat did, at least not until you own the company. Finally, be eccentric only because you truly want to. Otherwise, it only falls flat.

Corporate and Financial

If your goal is to reach the top of the corporate or financial ladder, then be prepared to dress in only the most conservative clothes. Most corporate presidents, bank presidents, and stockbrokers wear the conservative, traditional business dress described throughout this chapter. Beards and mustaches are barely tolerated in corporate board rooms, and any sign of flashiness is frowned upon and considered frivolous, if not effete, and cause for not promoting someone. Also, the leaders in the corporate and financial worlds seldom remove their jackets during the working day.

Law

What a lawyer wears depends upon the firm. There are some old-line, conservative firms that are more traditional than any business corporation. One young lawyer who went to work in a very conservative Wall Street firm was appalled to learn that no one removed his jacket and rolled up his sleeves during the work day.

Lawyers who spend a lot of time in courtrooms soon learn to dress for judges. One lawyer who earns over $100,000 a year said he always wore a slightly frayed white shirt for one particularly old-fashioned judge, who disliked rich lawyers. Many lawyers in large cities seem to have led the peacock movement in male dress, while others own closets full of traditional business suits. If you go to work for a law firm, take note—quickly—and dress the way everyone else does. Since lawyers deal with clients, senior partners keep an eagle eye on the dress habits of youngbloods. If you are shooting for a partnership, you simply cannot afford to dress differently from the older members.

Medicine

Among the professionals, doctors veer farthest from the traditional, conservative look, but doctors also experience very little pressure to conform to any standard of dress, as they basically work for themselves. Their sign of authority is the white office coat, and they seem to feel little need to use their other clothing to show power, so doctors frequently wear sports coats and casual slacks at work. Many doctors also wear short-sleeved shirts, since a longer sleeve could interfere with their work.

Sales

Sales is the most difficult category of all to describe because there are so many different areas. The best general guideline is to dress at least as well as your customers and to dress in the same style as they do.

Publishing, Advertising, and Art-related Fields.

Publishing, advertising, and art-related fields are the professions where a man can show a little individuality and even eccentricity in dress—and sometimes be rewarded for it. Wild ties, dark-colored shirts with beige suits, striped shirts with white collar and cuffs are all acceptable in these professions, once you have checked the atmosphere of the particular place in which you happen to work, which, like all other places of work, will have its own unwritten dress code. Dress is infinitely more individual in these professions.

CHAPTER 11

Dressing for Business: Women

M ICHAEL KORDA, author of two widely read business books, *Power* and *Success*, offers a list—albeit a somewhat personal one—of what women who want power and success should not wear in the office. His Index of Forbidden Objects includes:

glasses dangling from your neck on a chain
hats
high boots
white gloves (they make you look like a
    secretary from the 1940s)
harlequin glasses
sequins on anything
blue jeans
turbans
T-shirts with comic or pornographic messages printed on
    them
heavy dangling earrings

It is doubtful that Korda has seen sequins or harlequin glasses on a successful, gracious woman in the last twenty years. As for high boots and dangling earrings, they look spectacular and tasteful on some women. For most female executives, dressing is a matter of good taste, however, and the majority of items on Korda's list are not tasteful.

Perhaps the women who have come closest to finding the best way to dress as professionals are the ones who have had the courage to say no to the fashion designers in recent years and who have then gone on to develop their own highly individual looks.

Creating your own look involves studying the unwritten dress code where you work, just as any successful male would do, and dressing accordingly. It involves noticing class differences in the work world; secretaries and clerks do, in fact, dress differently from female executives. And creating an individual look involves buying the best clothes you can afford without looking too affluent for your salary.

Most women who have developed a comfortable look for work wear separates, in varying degrees of classical design. If you work in a high-fashion industry, in publishing, in art, or in other professions where eccentricity is tolerated, you will find it more acceptable to own and wear less conservative and even flamboyant outfits. Women working in banking and law dress more conservatively, as do women stockbrokers.

Suits are acceptable, as are blazers, silk shirts, and skirts that have been put together by an individual rather than by a clothing manufacturer. Pantsuits are acceptable on some occasions and, in many offices, so are good-looking slacks, a shirt, and a sweater or jacket.

More important than what you choose to wear is the ability to dress tastefully—in short, to show that you know the right thing to wear on any given occasion.

HOW NOT TO LOOK LIKE A SECRETARY

Discreet signals that say you know you belong at the top can be conveyed through dress. Secretaries and clerks, as a logical response to being young, tend to dress in campy, high style. In the 1970s, this meant platform shoes, jeans, T-shirts, and even, for a few too many years, miniskirts—all of which are obviously not right for a woman who aspires to be at the top.

On the other hand, too many woman executives tend to think that looking successful means dressing in stodgy, conservative clothes. If skirts are long one year, they wear theirs at a safe just-below-the-knee length; if skirts are short, they still wear theirs just below the knee. They wear the plainest black or brown pumps they can find year-round, even though strappy beige sandals might go better with their summer clothes. Plain suits and dresses often form the backbone of their wardrobes. This is a kind of look that just misses the mark, besides making its wearer look dull and uncreative.

For women as for men, the key to dressing for the profession is to dress for the particular office in which you work and to use the small status symbols that show you belong to your profession. (Moving yourself one step further into the upper class is, for some women in some professions, particularly dangerous. If you can afford designer clothes, most bosses will assume that you are not long for the work world.)

THE SIGNS OF STATUS

Status symbols have never had more power than they do today. For women, this means investing in Gucci shoes, Louis Vuitton purses, Cartier watches, and Cross pens. While any one or even all of these status symbols help to convey a success-oriented image, don't panic if you can't afford them. It is still possible to convey a professional, success-oriented look without investing in a single expensive, big-name status symbol.

For example, it is more important to carry a good leather purse than it is to carry a Vuitton. A gold pen may or may not be noticed by the top brass whom you seek to impress, while it *is* important to wear neutral colors such as beige, dark blues, browns, and grays—unless you live in the Deep South or a small town where bright colors are preferred despite your status. It is important to wear good wool or linen skirts or pants and wool or cashmere sweaters rather than polyester, pastel outfits. What does not matter one whit is where you buy your clothes so long as they manage to convey the look you need to get ahead.

Conservative shoes are a wise investment, but they should be stylish. In the same way that a man would not appear at work wearing hiking shoes with a suit if he knew how to dress, a woman headed for the top would not wear platform shoes in a bright color when an elegant beige or rust sandal with a little gold trim would convey her message more effectively.

SELECTION OF AN OUTFIT

Many women dress poorly because they do not know how to buy a well-fitting garment that is also well made. First, let us consider the matter of quality.

Not only are natural fibers such as cotton, linen, wool, and silk stylish, but also they are classic fabrics that are always acceptable. Still, linen can look very wrinkled five minutes after it is put on, and while wrinkles may be fine on the art gallery circuit these days, they have little to do with looking efficient at work. One way around the dilemma is to buy polyester blends, particularly for lighter-weight fabrics. But buy only polyester or polyester blends that look and feel like natural fibers. If you can't tell that a material is synthetic, chances are no one else will notice.

Quality has a lot to do with how well made a garment is. Look for seams that are wide enough to withstand the tension of normal wear and that also can be let out if necessary. Facings, too, should be fairly wide if they are not constantly to be flipping out at inopportune moments. The seams should be neatly and evenly sewn, particularly where stitching shows, such as at the cuffs and around the collar. The plainer a garment, however, the less likely that poor quality will be obvious, so if you want to buy an inexpensive blouse or shirt to go under your expensive new suit, look for a simple style.

Skirt length is another problem. Whether you want to stay with a conservative just-below-the-knee look or go with a high-fashion length is a matter of personal taste, as well as a matter of noting what is appropriate in your office or profession. Try to strike a happy medium without being afraid to show your individuality. If you like a new look but it is not being worn in your office, go ahead and try it and see what the reaction is.

CLOTHES THAT FIT

Fit is just as important in women's clothes as it is in men's. Smoothness is the key to good fit. A jacket, skirt, and especially pants should fit smoothly—not so tight that they wrinkle anywhere and not so loose that they bag. Pants especially need to fit well when they are part of an office outfit. Even if you have a beautiful body, tight pants are not the way to adorn it if you are serious about your work.

When having pants fitted, be sure to wear the shoes you plan to wear with them. Pants should break just slightly over the instep of the shoe and fall over the beginning of the heel in the back. Women's pants can be tailored in the same way as men's, that is, at a slight angle that is lower in back than in front, or they can be hemmed straight across. Just make sure they are long enough to look good with the shoes you plan to wear them with.

Sleeves should be smooth at the armhole, and free movement of the arms should not be hindered. Collars can also cause fitting problems; they should neither ride up nor pull away from your neck.

BUYING ACCESSORIES

Purses and Briefcases

A purse is the major accessory for most women. It may look extremely businesslike to carry only a briefcase—until you are in an important meeting with a client and your spare pair of panty hose pops out or a lipstick rolls across the floor. If you, like many women, find it awkward to carry a purse in addition to a briefcase or tote, one solution might be to buy a flat, envelope purse that can be tucked into your briefcase.

Your purse and briefcase should show that you mean business. Brown leather for a briefcase and any good leather for a purse is acceptable. Leather may be expensive, but it is worth every penny for the note of taste it adds to your look. This is the place to splurge if you can afford to.

Gloves

Gloves are not often worn merely for adornment these days. If you do wear gloves, choose a sporty-looking leather glove that adds pizazz to an outfit. Leather gloves, cashmere- or wool-lined for cold weather, are the best kind to buy for work wear. Avoid white cotton—it looks too prim. If you cannot afford good leather, knitted gloves are a nice substitute. If you can find a synthetic that looks like leather, buy it—just make sure the difference cannot be detected by the naked eye.

Hats

In cold climates hats are a necessity; most women coordinate them with their winter coats. Felt hats are the most popular. Knit hats are somewhat less acceptable, except in really cold weather when everyone lowers one's standards a little for the sake of keeping warm.

In warm climates or during the summer, a smart-looking straw hat is a good idea. Avoid head scarves, unless you work in a profession where they are appreciated, which excludes corporations, banks, and most businesses. They look too casual for these professions.

Shoes

Buy shoes to go with your outfits, rather than buying them at random and trying to make them work with your clothes. If you cannot afford many pairs, a good basic wardrobe of shoes consists of a pair of black or brown pumps, beige sandals, and possibly some black leather or patent leather sandals that can take you to work and out on the town. While you need not stick to plain pumps, buy shoes that are made of good leather and have very little trim (gold on the heels and vamps is the most acceptable).

High boots have become part of every woman's wardrobe these days, and there is no reason not to wear them at the office. There is every reason not to wear a pair of boots that is obviously intended for outdoor wear only. All-weather boots or sports boots or anything remotely resembling cowboy boots should either not be worn to work or should be taken off and replaced with pumps when you get there.

The days of coordinating shoes and purse are mostly gone. There is nothing wrong with doing it, but it is far better, if your budget is limited, to invest in one good leather purse that will go with everything. If your purse coordinates with anything, it should be with your winter coat; it need only blend with an outfit.

Coats

A winter coat should be of the best quality you can possibly afford, stylish but not of such high style that it cannot be worn for four or five years. Black is a good color if you will also wear the coat for evening wear. Otherwise stick to any tasteful color— brown, camel, rust, beige, dull green, navy, possibly red. If you find an inexpensive coat that looks great, buy it and then buy an expensive set of buttons to put on it; it will instantly make the coat look much better than it is. The life of a coat can be prolonged by relining, and any coat that has taken a hard winter of wear will surely need some lining repair. Never wear a coat with a torn lining or a missing button; it looks sloppy. Also regularly check a coat to make sure that the lining does not hang out from the coat in back; if it does, have this fixed before wearing the coat again.

Raincoats should look businesslike. This is one place where a direct imitation of your male colleagues would not hurt: buy a beige raincoat and carry a black umbrella. Resist the urge to go to bright colors in either an umbrella or a coat; they simply look too frivolous. You might consider buying a folding umbrella if, like most women, you are already burdened with a briefcase and a purse; the umbrella can be slipped inside either.

Fur coats are fine if you live in a cold climate. In recent years fur has moved from being the exclusive privilege of the rich to being available to many persons, so a modest fur (or even a not-so-modest one) no longer signals to your boss that you can do without your paycheck.

Jewelry

While there is no single piece of jewelry that is the mark of an innocent in quite the way that a class ring is on a man, a professional woman should wear conservative—and if at all possible, good—jewelry. Either gold or silver is fine, and yes, the two are mixed today in many interesting styles.

A watch is a necessity. One man reported that a woman who worked with him drove him crazy by showing up three or four times a day to ask what time it was. Granted, any man could choose not to wear a watch and pull this same stunt on his coworkers, but this man somehow saw her action as a sign that the woman was only interested in how soon she could wrap up her work day and move on to her social life.

A work watch should be fairly plain, either gold or silver or leather-banded. A diamond watch should be saved for evening;

diamonds and rhinestones, with the exception of those on engagement and wedding rings, are unacceptable, in fact, for daytime wear. Avoid any jewelry that looks too much as if it should be worn only for evening, even if the piece is made of precious stones. If you want to wear fancy jewelry after work, take it to work and put it on just before you leave.

CONCLUSION

Like a male executive, a woman needs to recognize the constrictions and unwritten dress codes of the office in which she works. While individuality is valued far more today than it was even ten years ago in offices, dressing to fit in does make you more promotable.

CHAPTER 12

For Women Only

A MAN who is a great supporter of women's rights has noted on numerous occasions his disdain of books that tell women they need special help, or that they need to do something differently from men in order to succeed. During one conversation about this subject, we were discussing a book that purported to tell women how to invest in the stock market, as if there were something women should do differently from men. The man's point seemed particularly well taken. And while we realize that this idea most certainly does not apply to every aspect of a woman's life in business, we still feel there is a certain wisdom in our friend's message. Therefore everything written thus far in this book has been directed to men and women equally, with little recognition of innate differences between the sexes.

But, of course, women in business, particularly those in positions of power, do have some special etiquette problems. For example, does a feminist female executive who feels strongly about equality make a point of not letting male colleagues show her the courtesies frequently shown to females? And if she decides such courtesies are not to be tolerated, how does she explain this to her male colleagues without destroying a working relationship she needs to survive?

THE LITTLE COURTESIES THAT HURT

It's often the little things, such as having a door held open or a cigarette lit, that are the most painful to a woman. Some women simply acquiesce in the name of getting ahead with the least amount of pain, while others feel they are sacrificing a principle if they permit men to offer them these small courtesies.

If you are among the latter, it is only polite to find a tactful way to tell a male colleague that you don't appreciate such attentions. A heavy hand is only alienating and rude. To make a point about holding doors, for example, you might deliberately hold a door open for one or more male colleagues. To avoid having your cigarettes lighted, which is admittedly a rather silly custom to uphold at work, simply have a lighter handy and do it yourself, even if you must accidentally neglect to see a proffered lighter. Spot the lighter *after* you have lighted your own cigarette and simply say, "Thank you, but I really prefer to light my own cigarettes these days." A colleague who refuses to pick up on this not-so-subtle hint is employing his own power tactics.

WHAT YOUR LANGUAGE SAYS ABOUT YOU

Most men today, unless they are very apolitical or very old, are aware of the connotations of terms such as "lady," "girl," and "woman." Most liberated women today have strong feelings about not being referred to by such patronizing terms as "girl" or "gal"; the problem is how to handle their use tactfully, and, as a last resort, rather impolitely if necessary.

First, consider the source of the problem and the cost of proving your point. If the chairperson of the board, who happens to be eighty years old, comments on what a fine young lady you are, do you really want to lecture him about your political views? And isn't there a possibility that you should consider deferring politely to his age, just as you would to that of any other aged person?

When your colleagues use derogatory terms, it is important to make it clear that you don't appreciate their use. Since most men today know what they are saying when they use such terms, they frequently make the mistake of following them with comments such as, "I suppose you are one of those women's libbers who doesn't like to be called a lady," or "I know it's in to say woman, but I still think of you as a lady." When you have such an obvious parry to counter, simply say, with your biggest smile, "That's right; I don't appreciate such language" or "I really do think I'm old enough to be called a woman." What you say isn't nearly as important as how you say it: with a smile and a light tone.

If you aren't given an opening by a colleague who persists in using such expressions around a hard-working woman, you can still smile and say, "I work awfully hard for a living, and I really would like to be referred to as a woman."

Numerous women reported that one or two honest but polite comments often are not enough to end the jibes, but there is nothing to stop you from always commenting that you do not appreciate being called a "girl"—over and over and over again.

WOMAN AS SERVANT

Women in meetings are still often expected to assume responsibility for bringing coffee or food. Women who have earned positions of responsibility have every reason to resent this, but again, it is easier to make a point politely. If someone is rude enough to ask you to get coffee or food, smile and say, "Sure." Then call out of the meeting room for a secretary and pass on the food and drink order to her or him. You probably won't be asked to provide food service again, and your point will have been made without rudeness to your boss or coworkers.

THE FEMALE EXECUTIVE AS SECRETARY

In the same way that men often assume that women have some innate ability to bring on the food and drink, they also assume that taking notes is a natural talent of all women, so unless you own the company, it is better to be prepared to ward off such requests graciously than to assume they won't occur.

The solution is simple, although it takes a little nerve and may surprise the men present. But don't worry about that: Business is mostly games—men know it and women know it—and if, once in a while, women have to create a few new games until the battle of the sexes has equalized somewhat more, so be it

If you are asked to take notes at a meeting, simply smile (again, it is more than a polite gesture; it deflects hostility), and say that you are not prepared to do so, not having brought a notepad of any kind with you. Generally your point will then be made; occasionally someone will be loutish enough to ask another man to give you his notepad. At this point, you must take a stand, albeit a politely phrased one. Look the person making the request straight in the eye and in your calmest, most disarming voice, say, "I really would feel uncomfortable being the one to take notes."

Another tactic is to say, "I think it would be better to have someone else do that." Then sit through what will seem like endless silence. If all else fails, or if you have been asked to take notes one too many times, when you are asked again, call a secretary to sit in and take notes. Need we say that this should be done with extreme politeness?

If these tactics are employed in a disarming, casual way, you probably won't get caught in a direct confrontation or power struggle. Few men today are looking for confrontations with what, in too many cases, are still their token female executives.

On the other hand, until it becomes obvious that you *are* being harassed, assume that any man asking you to do things that are not in keeping with your status is not doing so maliciously, and give him the benefit of the doubt until you learn otherwise.

With all these techniques, persistence is of the utmost importance. You simply will have to correct a boss or coworkers not
once but many times if you feel strongly about your rights. Try
always to do it graciously and in a way designed not to offend
someone you will still have to work with or for.

If a coworker does appear to be malicious in his intentions, then
it is time to treat his actions as you would those of any other
competitor. Techniques for this are discussed in Chapter 1.

INTIMACIES—ACCEPTING AND REJECTING THEM

Most instances of men touching women at work have an erotic
base. While a man may casually fling an arm around another
man's shoulder or pat him on the back, these actions usually don't
have the same intentions when directed toward women.

The way any woman handles sexual overtures is a highly
personal matter, but assuming that you want to maintain a degree
of professional distance and reject the pass, then try to find a
gracious way to do so. After all, it is flattering to be liked by
someone, and just because the someone happens to be a colleague
is no reason to take offense.

Often sexual overtures begin with flattery. There is a difference, as every man and woman knows, between a compliment
about how attractive one looks generally and how sexy one looks
specifically. Any woman's antennae should go up when she hears
the latter. Some men, entirely lacking in subtlety, make a physical
approach. If the come-on involves touching, you have a right to
remove whatever part of his body is touching yours. Usually it is
smart to follow this up with a statement that makes your position
very clear, such as, "I'm sorry, but I don't go for that sort of thing
at work." Then leave quickly; don't hang around for conversation
about where and when you *do* allow that sort of thing.

If a man persists in making sexual overtures in which you have no interest, you may have to give up the façade of politeness and tell him off. Try to do this out of earshot of others. Be friendly and polite the next time you see him, but don't overdo it, just as you wouldn't overdo making up with a competitor whom you had set straight on some other aspect of your working relationship.

The simplest overtures to handle are those from peers. What happens, though, when the sexual harassment comes from someone older and more powerful, like your boss? This is a situation that calls for special tact if you value your job. If persistent sexual overtures are made by a male superior, first try to find a flattering way to reject him. The best way to do this is to find a reason to say no that has nothing to do with him personally. You could simply say that you are already involved with someone else, although if this is untrue, it may come back to haunt you at odd times, like when the boss invites you to dinner and asks you to bring your friend. You could say that you are very involved in your work and have simply made it a rule never to go out with persons with whom you work. You could say that you are just getting over a sad affair and really don't feel like having a relationship with someone right now. Try to temper a rejection with an honest compliment if at all possible. (You can, of course, decide to take a man up on his sexual overtures—a not uncommon occurrence these days in many offices.)

LUNCH WITH COLLEAGUES

Perhaps the most challenging aspect of being a female executive is forging relationships with peers. Let's face it, men tend to form bonds with each other, and rarely do they do this better than at work.

It is usually up to a woman who wants—and for business reasons, needs—to break into these groups to take the initiative in establishing the kind of working relationships she needs. If your colleagues seem shy about asking you to join them at lunch, ask them to join you. And as in any other situation, set the tone for the way you would like to be treated during lunch. If you prefer to remove your coat without assistance, do so quickly, out of range of those who might help. If you don't want someone to pull out a chair for you when you sit down, seat yourself promptly upon reaching the table. (On the other hand, if a maître d'hotel is planning to seat you, it is rude to ignore his attempts. After all, it is part of his job to provide this service to women, and while you may have a chance and a reason to reform your coworkers, it is simply not appropriate to do the same for the waiters of the world.)

Many men feel awkward about letting a woman pay for a meal. And many women feel even more awkward about not paying for themselves, especially when they are with their colleagues. Female executives report that there are two approaches to this problem. The first, and gentlest, one is to play a waiting game. Always offer to pay, but don't argue about it. Eventually, most men who lunch regularly with a female coworker will relent, if only to salvage their own budgets.

The second approach is equally polite, although slightly more aggressive. Simply insist that you want to pay your share. Take money out of your purse and give it to the person you are with or place it on the table in a way that indicates that you will indeed walk away leaving a $10 tip for an $8 lunch unless the money is used for your share of the bill.

As a last resort, if a man persists in trying to pick up the tab for lunch, gently explain how awkward you find this situation and that you will have to stop having lunch with him if he does not let you pay. He will probably relent and breathe a secret sigh of relief.

The exception to paying your own way is when lunching with your boss, who may ask male and female colleagues to lunch and treat. It is only gracious to accept this gesture.

Unless this really matters to you, who pays for what is not really worth making an issue over the first couple of times someone offers to pay. Old manners do die hard, and even the most liberated man may feel he has to make the gesture of offering to pay when he does not know a female colleague well. Such men often willingly let a woman pay for herself, or even treat occasionally, after one or two lunches, so the situation is best handled by not making an issue of it until it is obvious that a man is making a chauvinistic gesture rather than exercising manners he has not quite been able to let go of.

CLIENT RELATIONSHIPS

Most of the gestures that a woman uses to handle colleagues can readily be applied to relationships with clients or customers. Set the tone for the way you expect to be treated and make your feelings clear without hurting anyone else's.

Often a male client or customer is slightly ill at ease about how to treat a high-powered executive who happens to be a woman, so he is eager to follow her lead. Showing overt feminism in the presence of a traditional-minded man may jeopardize your working relationship, however, so give careful consideration to any politicking you decide to do while you are conducting business. Is it worth risking the loss of an account to make a point about feminism?

About the only major hurdle that women encounter with male customers today occurs when the bill arrives. Numerous women reported solving this problem through the use of a credit card. For some reason, if men do not see money, they do not get as nervous about having a meal bought by a woman. A credit card is also a definite signal that the company is paying, and not the woman, and that suits most men just fine. If the waiter places the check beside the man, simply reach over and pick it up. If you frequently go to the same place for lunch, the waiters should quickly learn that you are to be given the check. If they don't, then you should talk with the manager.

HOW TO GET CREDIT FOR WORK

A common complaint with junior-level female executives, particularly those who have come up from the secretarial ranks, is that their superiors frequently take credit for work they have done. If you want to get ahead, however, your work must be noticed by top management. Therefore, it is important to get credit for the work you do.

You can ensure getting credit by putting your name on your work in a prominent place. A more tactful ploy with a boss who consistently fails to recognize your work is to draw up a list of responsibilities and take it in to the boss, seemingly to ask his or her advice about how you are allotting your time and what your priorities are. Such a list will force the boss to take an objective look at what you actually do—and, one would hope, to see that credit has not been given to you for doing it. If the oversight is accidental, you will probably find yourself gaining due recognition in short order. If the oversight is due to the boss's own insecurity, however, it may continue, and you may have to find another way to combat it, or even find another job.

PROBLEMS WITH OTHER WOMEN

Not infrequently a female executive may find that her worst enemies at work are those members of her own sex who are jealous of the power she has attained. Clerical workers can do considerable damage in sabotaging someone's work if they put their minds to it. An additional factor that may create tension is the college-educated woman who got stuck at the clerical or low-management level and resents someone with a similar education moving ahead more quickly, as frequently happens these days.

Handling this situation is not unlike walking a tightrope. You should be the one to take the initiative in setting the tone for these relationships, and it requires tact. Because you are also a woman, one would hope you would find considerable empathy to use as a base in establishing relationships with female clerks and secretaries. Anyone who has ever served time in the clerical ranks should not have too much of a problem recalling the things that were most degrading. It is then a relatively simple matter to refrain from doing those things: asking a secretary to get coffee all the time and never returning the favor; insisting on unrealistic deadlines that may infringe on a secretary's personal life; and even expecting a secretary to interrupt the work he or she is presumably doing for you to make a telephone call that you could just as easily make youself.

On the other hand, you do have executive responsibilities, and it is important that you exercise them. Do not make your secretary's life so visibly easy, out of sympathy for his or her plight, that your actions are noted by your colleagues and superiors, thus gaining you a reputation for being unnecessarily soft.

Avoid socializing excessively with subordinates (unless it's the rule where you work), not because you do not respect them as persons, but because persons normally socialize with their peers at work. Rather than seeming rude to the secretaries, maintaining some distance will tend to make everyone feel more at ease.

And speaking of easing a secretary's way, while you are showing respect for clerical work, make sure that you are truly respecting *that* work. Realize early on that some secretaries do not aspire to executive positions and take great pride, quite justifiably, in doing clerical work. It is rude to assume that every female clerk who comes through your office door wants to become your protégé and follow in your footsteps to the executive washroom.

Showing a normal amount of empathy and enlisting clerical workers as your allies, plus waiting through the inevitable period when they are taking your measure, has often won a tactful female executive better relationships with other women in the office than any man can ever hope to attain.

Your Attitude

One way to get equal treatment from colleagues is to expect to get it. Don't let yourself resort to ploys, manipulations, or any other of the tactics by which men and women have frequently guided their personal relationships. Create an aura that makes it clear that you expect equal treatment from your colleagues.

Just as important as creating this attitude is the need to fit in with a company. It is not a coincidence that lawyers in one law firm all lean toward wearing their hair the same length and wearing gray pin-striped suits. For years men have sustained their power structures through the use of such visible signals to one another. It is easy, therefore, to imagine the threat presented by a woman executive who can and does wear pastel colors, carries a purse in addition to a briefcase, and does not wear her hair at all like any of her male colleagues. Although many articles and books have recently suggested that women try to look as much like the men they work with as possible, we do not advocate such an approach, on the grounds that it is slightly ridiculous and can actually be a detriment to your image as a woman. Even if a woman buys a gray pin-striped suit, it is a pretty sure bet that she won't look quite like one of the men. And if she cuts her hair like theirs, she may even find herself out of a job. So what is the solution for a woman willing to fit in with the look of her company or business?

Compromise. Pick up on the mood of the company, just as any ambitious young male executive would do. If it is indeed a gray pin-striped kind of place, buy conservative clothes, jewelry, and accessories. Studies have shown that women tend to choose quieter, less colorful clothing and accessories as they gain more power, and one wonders if this is perhaps a subconscious way of handling the "company look." At any rate, do dress in keeping with the mood of the place where you work.

In addition, follow the company line in manners and operating methods as much as you can without sacrificing your sense of identity. This is, after all, how men climb the corporate ladder, and it behooves any woman who wants to make her way to the top to do the same.

A FINAL WORD

Although these approaches may seem too soft to hard-core feminists, hard-core feminism is not the subject of this book— etiquette is. And etiquette is finding a way to get along graciously with others, which may in the long run be a far better way to handle even a hostile and unfair working situation.

CHAPTER 13

Landing That Big Job:
The Etiquette of
the Job Search

J OB HUNTING is not unlike a ritual dance. The chances of
getting a highly desired job increase greatly when you know
the correct pattern of steps. If you don't know the steps, or blindly
break the pattern, your chances diminish; you will have ruined an
opportunity to get the job you want. But, as in all instances where
actions are guided by etiquette, once you know the rules you can
use them—or not use them—to your advantage.

It is not the purpose of this book to provide the reader with
every detail concerning a job change. There are many excellent
books that deal in depth with how to handle an interview, a
headhunter, salary negotiations, and other aspects of job hunting.
This chapter will show you how to handle the etiquette of the job
search. It will show you how to develop the poise and tact necessary to get the job you truly want.

EXPANDING AND USING CONTACTS

Once you make the decision to look for another job, it's an
accepted practice to call business acquaintances and ask for help.
This is not a time to rely only on friends, and it is definitely not a

time to rely on colleagues with whom you work, unless you are very sure they can be trusted. Call or write to anyone who you think might be useful. If you are hesitant about calling someone you do not know well, remember that people like to help each other and that you can return a business favor at a later date. Besides, everyone likes to feel powerful, and passing on an important job lead to someone is a way of showing one's power.

Never give someone as a reference without checking with him or her first. And try to keep in touch with persons whom you plan to use as references. A call out of the blue after five years of no contact may not produce as glowing a reference as a call that is simply part of your routine of keeping up with old business friends.

Call any employment agencies or headhunters who have ever expressed an interest in you. Call suppliers, clients, old bosses, the person you met at a party last week who had some interesting business ideas.

When you talk to these people, just mention that you are beginning to look around. Note that there is no rush, that you have not mentioned this to anyone with whom you presently work and do not plan to, and that you would like to hear if anything interesting turns up. Be polite and low-keyed about your request for help.

News of most executive-level jobs are passed by word of mouth before they are listed in advertisements, but this is no reason to leave any stone unturned in the search. Read the ads in newspapers and trade journals and papers regularly. (Read them, however, at home or very discreetly at the office; it is surprising how often a sudden interest in the trade journal with the best ads will tip off others to your plans.)

Whenever you can, shoot higher than your present job level in using contacts. Just as you can improve your tennis game when you play with a slightly better player, you can find tips about higher-level jobs from someone with a more prestigious position.

USING EXECUTIVE PLACEMENT SERVICES

The key to using executive placement services is to do just that—use them. Executive recruitment services fall into two general categories. One kind takes a sum of money from you in return for marketing you to companies. The fee ranges from several hundred dollars to several thousand dollars. While many of these agencies are reputable, the fact is that they have already gotten their money and will have less of a stake in finding employment for you. If you use a company like this, or any recruitment company, for that matter, be sure you have checked its reputation very carefully before you enlist its services in your behalf.

The second kind of recruitment company takes its fee from the company that eventually hires you; needless to say, this company has more of a stake in finding work for you. Such recruitment organizations work at all levels of business; some place persons only in the $40,000-plus salary range; other executive recruitment firms start with a salary range as low as $12,000, and some have no minimum salary.

There is another way in which this type of firm can be selective. In the more elite firms, referrals are always made through contacts. If you want to establish a contact with one of these firms, make a few discreet inquiries among acquaintances to see who has used such a recruitment agency and would be willing to let you use his or her name when you call. Once you have the name of someone who is known to the agency, call him or her, introduce yourself, and ask if you can drop a résumé in the mail or make an appointment to talk. (Occasionally, one of these agencies will obtain your name and will contact you to see if you are interested in changing jobs. Even if you decline, make a note for future reference of the person to whom you talked as well as the name of the agency.)

Executive recruitment agencies tend to devote more time and effort to candidates who are qualified for high-paying executive positions. At the lower salary levels, there is a point of diminishing returns in the amount of time they can invest. This is something any executive should be aware of. One way to counter diminishing interest is to make it clear that you are using more than one recruitment service and that you are actively looking on your own.

There is a tendency among executive recruitment agencies, as among other types of employment agencies, to offer a client a job that may not exactly match his or her needs or interests. Such offers need only be politely declined, although there is an interesting counterploy that helps to keep an agency interested when you must decline a job they have suggested. Tell them you have a counteroffer involving more money or a position that is exactly what you want. If the service is highly interested in selling you, and stands to gain a good-sized fee from doing so, it will work a little harder and faster to place you.

There is a particular time in your career when executive recruitment agencies are especially useful, and that is when you hope to make a sizeable jump in salary. Since there is always a chance that a prospective employer will contact your present company to check on your salary, among other things, there is a special safeguard in letting an executive recruitment agency represent you. Prospective employers assume the agency has done all the checking that needs to be done; therefore you have a slightly freer hand in exaggerating your present salary. One young executive, for example, who was grossly underpaid at $13,500 and wanted a large salary jump, was marketed at $20,000 by an executive employment agency.

In dealing with executive recruitment agencies, play fair but play with your self-interest in mind, and they will frequently be of help to you as you climb to the top.

OBTAINING AN INTERVIEW

Once you have sent out initial feelers and answered a few ads, making appointments for interviews will be the next step. In obtaining an interview, always go directly to the person with the power to hire. This is usually your prospective boss—a boss being, by loose definition, the person who can get you a promotion or a raise and who can hire and fire you. Especially at the executive level, it is important to avoid the personnel office of a company. Going through personnel is a giveaway that you lack contacts or are not aggressive enough to pick up the phone and get through to the person who *can* hire you.

Some interviewers make the mistake of lecturing prospective employees on the nature of the company; a skilled interviewer will let you tell him or her what you know about the place, so never go to an interview without first having done some homework. Know something about the company's history, its profit picture, its image, and its future plans. A word of warning, though: all this information should come from public sources. Even if your best friend or old college roommate works there and has personally introduced you, never admit to knowing anything about the inner politics or workings of a company during a job interview.

Dressing for the Interview

Always dress appropriately for an interview, even though this means different things in different cities, companies, and professions. As a rule of thumb, plan to dress as you would if you were going to work—only slightly more conservatively. A woman who might ordinarily wear a silk shirt and linen skirt to work might want to add a jacket. A man who wears a suit should pick his best-looking and most conservative one for a job interview. All professions have unspoken dress codes, however, as do individual companies. For example, if you want a job in a hot Madison Avenue advertising company, your efforts may well be facilitated by showing up for the interview in a mauve shirt and a wild tie.

Whatever you do, do not dress casually for an interview. Under no circumstances should you wear jeans or corduroys—even if they are what you would wear daily were you to get the job. One of the unwritten rules of the interview is that the prospective employee must appear immaculate and totally pulled together for the interview. If the weather is bad, wear boots and change to clean shoes when you arrive at the company for the interview. If you discover a loose button on a coat as you are heading out the door for the interview, put on another coat. A lost button, unshined shoes in need of reheeling, or dirty or broken fingernails all can and will be held against you when you are seeking a job. They will be seen as reflections of your ability to do your work satisfactorily.

KNOWING THE ETIQUETTE OF THE INTERVIEW

When job hunting, it is important to display the fact that you know how to behave among civilized company. After all, the entire ritual of job hunting is designed to show that you know the etiquette of the world of work. Here is a list of rules that will help you on any job interview:

1. Try to make a good impression on everyone with whom you come in contact, especially the secretary or receptionist who greets you. The person who interviews you may well ask his or her opinion of you, or he or she may even decide to offer an unsolicited opinion, particularly if you were not overly polite.
2. You must arrive on time. There is simply no excuse one can offer, short of a national disaster, for being late for an interview to obtain a job that one seemingly wants very much.
3. Make the first move to shake hands, or be prepared to make the first move. Until recently, etiquette books recom-

mended that the prospective employee should always wait for an interviewer to offer his or her hand, but that issue has become more complicated today, mostly due to the arrival of women into positions of executive power. Traditionally, a man has waited for a woman to extend her hand. There is a simple solution for men and women: as the interviewee, extend your hand immediately upon meeting the person who will interview you. It is always a gracious gesture to make toward another person, and it can also be taken as a sign that you have leadership qualities.

4. If you have some time in the reception area before the interview begins, ask if you may hang up your coat. You will look more at ease if you go into the interview with as little extra baggage as possible. If you are ushered into the interviewer's office immediately, wait until he or she asks if you want to remove your coat and indicates where to put it.

5. Men remove hats when they enter a building, and women keep their hats on. Gloves should be removed by either sex before shaking hands with someone, particularly if they are of the bulky winter variety.

6. Unless you are greeted with a very obvious power tactic, such as a long, ongoing phone conversation or a long wait in someone's office, do not sit down until you are asked to do so.

7. Do not smoke or chew gum or, for that matter, accept candy, even if if is offered. Any of these activities will detract from your effectiveness as a speaker.

8. Whether or not to call someone by a first name can pose a problem these days. Generally it is better not to use first names unless the interviewer indicates that it is preferred. If an interviewer calls you by your first name, do not assume this is permission to do the same. In fact, it is always safest at the interview stage to use "Mr.," "Mrs.," or "Ms." And don't make a point of asking a woman whether she is a

"Mrs.," "Miss," or "Ms." This has been worked to death. Call all women "Miss" (or "Ms.," if you prefer), and let the woman take the initiative of using "Mrs." if that is her preference.

9. Once you are seated, do not fidget. Sit up straight without seeming stiff and look directly at the interviewer.

10. Listen intently. When ready to answer a question, it is sometimes effective to take a moment or two to ponder the answer. It will make you look thoughtful and make your answers appear more meaningful and less as if they have been prepared in advance, which, of course, they have been.

11. Exhibit self-confidence, but be careful not to turn the interview into an ego trip. The person interviewing you is trying to determine one thing—how much use you will be to his or her company. Remember this and try to keep your answers to any questions pertinent.

12. Look for signals that the interview is ending and make a graceful exit. The interviewer may say, "It has been especially pleasant talking with you," or, "We will be in touch with you," or he or she may simply rise. Thank the interviewer, shake hands, and if you feel the interview has gone well, inquire whether you can call soon or ask when a decision can be expected. If the interview has gone so well that you feel you are a prime candidate for the job, you may graciously express your interest and desire to work for the company, but be careful not to overdo any flattery. A flashy display of false flattery as you exit may only give the person interviewing you second thoughts.

RECOGNIZING INTERVIEW TACTICS—THEIRS AND YOURS

Most interviewers have some sort of strategy. Their most important goal, of course, is to evaluate what you can do for the company. On another level, though, an interviewer will be testing how aggressive you are, how you handle stress, how high your anxiety level is, how you handle an awkward situation and, most important, how well you will fit in and how valuable you will be.

Almost everyone has heard stories of interviewers' deliberately entrapping an interviewee. The most famous of these is the version of the interviewer who offers a cigarette to an unsuspecting person who accepts it and then has to flounder for an ash tray—for there is none in the room. Actually it would be nice if all such tactics were so obvious. Unfortunately, the more important the job you are seeking, the subtler the tests you must undergo.

If you really want to know what is going on in an interview, an excellent book on the subject is *The Evaluation Interview* by Richard A. Fear. Mr. Fear discusses in detail such matters as seeming to take the interviewee into one's confidence as a means of getting him or her to open up and confess things he or she would not ordinarily divulge; staring piercingly; raising the eyebrows; or using other body language that will make the interviewee so ill at ease that he or she may begin to chatter—and in the course of chattering divulge information that is best kept to oneself.

There are several other good books on this subject that are worth reading if you want to bone up on the psychological tactics that can and will be used against you; check the local library for them. In this book we are concerned with the etiquette of counter-tactics to these techniques.

Being Ignored or Kept Waiting

What appears to be a case of bad manners exhibited by the person who is going to interview you may actually be a test of your patience. If an interviewer keeps you waiting, take the nearest chair (in his or her office, if that is where you have been asked to sit), pull out a magazine or, better yet, a crossword puzzle, and start to work. If you opt for reading, avoid a serious trade journal and stick instead with something such as *Time* or *Newsweek*. After all, there is not need to overdo this ploy, which has the effect of presenting you as a self-possessed and hard-to-ruffle person.

Do the same thing if an interviewer is engaged in what appears to be a lengthy phone call (first, though, allow him or her a few minutes on the phone in case this is not a ploy). It is polite to show no signs of having overheard a conversation, even if it occurs 2 feet away from you. Unless you are asked to, in fact, do not participate in any miscellaneous conversations that interrupt the interview. Your advice will be needed only after you are hired.

Answering Personal and Financial Questions

You do not have to answer personal or financial questions, but your best bet is to have a tactful reply ready for the interviewer who *does* ask. Generally, these questions are put to you in loose terms: "I suppose your divorce was an upsetting experience?" or "Wow, with interest rates the way they are, I can imagine what you got held up for when you bought that house." In response to questions like these, which the interviewer knows he or she has no business asking, your best bet is to laugh and say something vague such as, "Well, yes, I suppose so" or "Well, possibly that was the case." If you can carry it off, the ultimate way to deflect a personal question that you don't wish to answer is to smile and say nothing.

Answering Open-ended Questions

Be prepared to handle open-ended questions, for they are a favorite tactic of the interviewer seeking to put you so much at ease that you succumb to saying things you might not otherwise divulge. A comment such as, "My, you are young to have accomplished so much," has far more beneath the surface than meets the eye and requires a carefully planned answer. To acknowledge such a comment too modestly and quietly shows a lack of aggressiveness, and to answer it at great length may open the way for you to say a lot of things about your achievements that you never wanted to say. Try something such as: "Thank you, I'm glad you feel that way. Actually, I think what helped me most was my ability to . . ." Go on to describe one strong trait about yourself and then wrap up your answer.

Open-ended questions are often used to start someone talking about a problem area such as a poor work record, an extended period of unemployment, a personality clash with a boss, a reason for leaving a job, or an explanation for being fired. Fortunately, you know more about the flaws of your work record than does anyone else, so go into an interview with a ready answer to use in reply to such questions.

For example, an interviewer might say, "I suppose you were upset over being fired?" or "I assume that you enjoyed your six-month break from work?" In the former case, explain without rancor what the problem was, minimizing it as much as possible, and making yourself look good. Never lie about what happened, and never show bitterness toward others you have worked for. You might, for example, consider saying: "I felt bad that there was a personality clash. I've thought a lot about what precipitated it, and I feel it was basically a difference of opinion in management techniques. I suppose my fault was in wanting to move forward too fast . . ."

In the latter case, explain what you did during a period of unemployment that makes you a more useful employee—perhaps you took a special course on entertaining clients at home at Harvard Business School, researched a book on modern management methods, or wrote articles for business journals. Make it clear that you were not sleeping late or job hunting sporadically, that you were not only seriously job hunting but also keeping yourself busy with an important project.

Countering the Ultimate Tactic

Occasionally one encounters out-and-out rudeness in an interview. Be careful; it may only be a test. The appropriate reaction—if you think you want the job—is no reaction at all. Just continue displaying your good manners and hope that the boor who is not displaying his or hers is only making a small-scale power play and is not always so rude.

PLAYING DOWN HUMOR

Humor generally has little place in a job interview, but it is especially important not to be flip over what may be a potential problem area for you or for a future employer. Never laugh off having taken several months to find a job. Everyone knows these are not funny events in anyone's life, and you will only look flip or phony if you attempt to make light of them.

Speaking of the role of humor in the job-hunting process, humor is not a quality that will particularly impress a potential employer. An interviewer may tell a joke to put an interviewee at ease and it is certainly polite to laugh at that joke or comment about it, but it is not necessary to offer another joke as a rejoinder.

Many a young executive has come out of a job interview feeling that everything went extremely well simply because he or she and the interviewer laughed and joked with each other. Invariably, the interviewer is at that very moment disqualifying the prospective employee because she or he simply did not seem serious or dedicated enough to handle the job. Work—especially to the person who pays you—is deadly serious.

ACTING LIKE A TEAM PLAYER

Most interviewers will be trying to take your measure as a team player. When you hear questions about teamwork, it is important to speak well of your colleagues, as well as of the company you presently work for. Specific comments and compliments about the company you are hoping to go to work for are also a good way to convey the impression that you will be a loyal team player. You might, for example, comment that the interviewer's company has always been well known to you for its early innovations in team organization, or that it is known to most outsiders as a company that is good to its employees. Ask questions about the corporate structure that show you will welcome the opportunity to work with others closely. Describe team projects or other examples of cooperative work projects that you have been involved with in the past.

SHOWING OFF PERSONAL STRENGTHS GRACIOUSLY

An interviewer may attempt to get you to disclose personal traits that show you will be an asset to his or her company or to show a glaring personal weakness. Blunt questions may be asked about your personal finances or energy level and about whether you prefer status quo or enjoy having to cope with new situations. The "correct" answers to these are that you pay your bills promptly and are very responsible about personal debt; you have a great deal of energy and actually welcome the opportunity to expend a fair amount of it at work; and you always love a challenge.

No matter how honest you are, do not fall into the trap of admitting personal traits that might be deemed undesirable by a potential employer. Personal victories—conquering alcohol or drugs, overcoming a heavy debt load—may well come out later if you take the job, but there is no reason to mention them during the interview. In the same vein, personal problems—such as the fact that you are going through a harrowing divorce or that it is a major accomplishment for you to make it to work on time—should be glossed over if they even come up. Acknowledging them during an interview may cost you the job, so resist the temptation. And remember that an interviewer may come on as an extremely understanding and sympathetic person when he or she brings up these subjects; you will be tempted to open up just because of the aura of sympathy that is created. The interviewer may even bring up his or her own personal problems as a means of getting you to talk about yours. Be polite, be empathic, but do not admit to your personal problems or weaknesses.

While you are ducking these little stinging arrows of the skilled interviewer, make an effort to convey your strengths. Be gracious and modest as you do this, however. Most important is to try a little polite aggression. And note the use of the word "polite." Too often it does not seem to go with the word "aggression," yet polite aggression is the key to coming on strong without threatening another person. Aggression shows force, ambition, and clear thinking, all of which are traits that any company seeks in its executives. In a survey recently taken by the National Personnel Associates, an organization of independent recruiters with agencies in 131 cities, *lack of aggression* ranked number 20 out of twenty two reasons that persons frequently lose out on jobs. Disinterest and unresponsiveness was a major reason for not getting a job, ranking number 7 on the list of disqualifying reasons. With this in mind, a small aggressive act may obviously be called for. One executive reports that he hovers behind a prospective employee for several minutes, knowing it is annoying. He is waiting for a person who is aggressive enough to tell him that this is distracting. The easiest way to show aggression is to talk money and company policies. If the interview is going well, and both parties are showing interest in each other, then it is time to ask about salary ranges—not what you will get paid, but what the general range is, what the opportunities for promotion are, when and how reviews are made. It is not particularly wise to ask about vacation pay, days off, and other benefits at this stage. Talking money shows that you are concerned with finances, and what company isn't? A final word: when you talk money, be discreet. Do not, for example, disclose an unlimited family supply of gold should you be lucky enough to have one. Employers generally want to think that you need them, and they may fear that you will be too independent if they know you have no financial need for the job.

TALKING ABOUT PROBLEM AREAS

There may be some problem areas in your job history that emerge during the interview. Stay calm when the subject is brought up. One woman senior executive had to explain why her career was cut short at a bank when she got a superior who simply did not like women and who made it obvious that he would do nothing to promote her career. She resigned to look for another job full-time. When she was confronted with this seemingly rash move, she had a ready answer that served her well:

> Frankly, it became obvious from the new executive vice president's treatment of me and the other women working under him that he was not favorably disposed to women in business. While I tried not to let it bother me personally, it eventually caused several other women and me to look for new positions.

> Since a key promotion that I had been working toward steadily for eleven years was obviously not going to be in the offing, and since I had saved enough to support myself, I decided to resign and devote myself full-time to looking for a new, more challenging position.

This woman made her point so well—and she also had to explain why she was not given a good reference by the executive vice-president—that she soon had three very tempting offers in banking.

TELLING LITTLE LIES—WHEN AND HOW

Job hunting invariably involves some white lies or maybe even gray lies, since they are not told to salve anyone's ego, but rather, as a maneuver to get you what you want. One lie you will have to tell is about the amount of money you are making (assuming that you are looking to receive a substantial increase). Another white lie or two may have to be told to the persons with whom you currently work, for example, when you miss a day of work to go on an interview.

Let us consider the latter instance first. Secrecy at work is of the utmost importance to your present job security. Job-hunting time is, sad to say, a time to trust no one where you work. Just go out and find a better job, and then come back and tell your coworkers and your boss. Jobs probably create even stranger bedfellows than do politics, and it is deceptively easy, particularly when you have displayed equally good manners to everyone with whom you work and have respected their confidences, to assume that they will show you the same courtesy. Resist the urge to think along these lines for your own self-protection, and tell no one about your plans to change jobs until they are a *fait accompli*. When you must take a day or several hours off, give some polite excuse.

The other lie you will probably tell is about your salary. Executives who hire and executive recruitment agencies all admit that lying about one's present salary is a common practice. The amount you exaggerate by varies with your salary range and with the kind of contact you have with a prospective employer. Employees in the lower executive ranks, earning from $15,000 to $20,000, generally add 10 to 15 percent; executives in the upper echelon may tack on an extra 20 to 30 percent. An executive recruitment agency may increase a salary by more than an individual would; once an agency represents a client, there is little likelihood that a prospective employer will do anything to doublecheck a salary, so there is very little chance of getting caught. Also, executive recruitment agencies know the salary range a company is willing to pay, which makes it even easier to exaggerate a prospective employee's salary.

There is only one time when you are liable to be caught exaggerating a salary, and that is when you are unemployed. If you are still at your present job, it is a courtesy for the prospective employer not to check on you there. This means he or she will call only references who would have no idea what you are presently earning. Furthermore, many companies today refuse to release salary information, as well as any other personal information about employees, past and present.

Best of all, of course, is to maneuver yourself into a position where you do not have to state your present salary, but rather can say that you will need $35,000 or $48,000 or something in the "high 20s." Be bold and state your salary needs when the discussion on money starts. If the interviewer was going to offer substantially less, he or she may well go to a higher power in the corporation to check on the possibility of meeting your salary requirements if you have become a desirable prospect. Another reason to state your salary demands up front is that once the interviewer has announced a range far below what you can accept, it may be impossible to negotiate a compromise very far upward.

Some persons who have perfectly good common sense in all other areas of their careers lament the need to lie to a present or prospective employer. A truly ambitious person, however, usually knows it is the best way to get what he or she wants and to protect personal career interests. If you have difficulties with your conscience, then mentally put these falsehoods in the white-lie category that so often helps one out of an awkward social situation. Most well-mannered persons think nothing of telling a white lie designed to protect a friend or an acquaintance. Think of yourself as a friend and lie about your salary and your whereabouts to your prospective and present employers respectively.

LOOKING FOR THAT FIRST JOB

Choosing your first real job is an extremely important task, particularly if you are embarking on a career that will not offer you many opportunities for change. It is important to find a job that suits you and offers a challenging learning situation, one where you can be happy for several years. Too often, persons do not hold out for the best possible job and find themselves wasting several years that can never be recaptured. The ages for reaching an executive position decrease every year. Today many companies feel a young person should be in a good solid executive position by his or her thirties, and many persons expect to reap rewards at an earlier age.

Among your contacts, make sure to count the placement office of your college or university. Take care always to treat the persons working there as cordially as you would any prospective employer. It is especially thoughtful to send them a note thanking them for their services when you find a job. Most college and university placement services are set up to help graduates who have been out of school for several years, so this is one more base to be covered when a job hunt is started.

School placement offices often have lists of companies at which their alumni are employed, and these can prove to be helpful contacts. If you are interested in a company, it is sometimes helpful to contact an alumnus of your school who works there to ask whether he or she will take a little time to sit down and talk with you. After meeting you, the person may well decide to give you a hand in your search for a job.

If you feel any nervousness about interviews (and who hasn't at one time or another?), set up some practice interviews with companies in your field that you are not particularly interested in working for. Interviewing is something one gets better at with practice.

The comment you will probably hear most often during interviews is that you lack the specific experience needed for the job. This is not the time to bow your head and walk quietly away. You will get an extra ten points, and possibly the job, if you have a ready response that points out some factor in your training or background that could be put to work on the job, or if you point out some personality traits that would work for you in the position you seek.

Some executives find that job hunting only increases their sense of competitiveness and makes their blood flow faster; others dread the entire process. Regardless of your personal feelings, play the game according to the rules of etiquette and you will greatly increase your chances of coming out on top. And remember, it is just a game—a game played according to rules that any intelligent person can master with a little practice.

KNOWING POST-INTERVIEW ETIQUETTE

One very small action guaranteed to win anyone extra points is to follow up an interview with a thank-you note. Since this is still basically a business transaction, the note may be typed and should be written on your business letterhead—your personal one, that is, not the one of the company you presently work for. Thank the person for taking the time to see you and perhaps add a kind comment or two about the company and how you hope to be hearing from them soon. Try not to write more than one paragraph, or the note may begin to look either pandering or social.

TALKING SALARY AND BENEFITS

For most executives, the most important decision about a new job is what the salary will be. Whereas many executives a few years ago would move for an increase of 20 to 25 percent, 35 to 40 percent is now the more usual guideline.

Beyond this, benefits fall into two categories: those that are obviously business-related and need to be worked out as part of the formal job arrangement, and those that are "extras," which may only be hinted at and are never formally offered during hiring talks. Any executive selling a company's image naturally learns to drop any of the latter kinds of benefits into conversations during the hiring process. One might, for example, mention the company condominium in Florida and how much fun he or she had last winter fishing there with the company's top clients. A company airplane, trips to Europe, vacation homes, sporting events, and any special company-sponsored trips are benefits worth dropping into a conversation, although they are not normally offered to a prospective employee in any formal sense.

Benefits that *are* discussed include insurance programs, pension plans, stock options, bonuses, incentive payments, lifetime consulting fees, cars used in business, and any financial arrangements required to help an employee make a move. Sometimes a company will offer to assume responsibility for a mortgage on a house that an employee must sell if he or she is going to relocate, or a company will agree to buy back a house the employee bought when he or she relocated, if and when the employee leaves the company. Club memberships may or may not be mentioned; these are relatively small benefits in terms of the money involved, but they do involve a certain amount of status, and membership in certain clubs may go with certain executive positions.

A prospective employee need not be a passive bystander in discussions of benefits; you are, after all, striking a deal for your future. You will never be in a stronger bargaining position, for a corporation is never more flexible than during the hiring process. Once you are part of the organization, all sorts of loopholes can be found for not giving you what you want or what you think you have earned, but when a company is wooing you, it wants you and knows it is going to have to give a little to get you, and any smart, ambitious executive should take full advantage of this opportunity. After all, you have nothing to lose. Rarely does the hiring process break down for lack of agreement about salary and benefits.

Go into the final interview with a clear idea of what you want, what you would like to have, and what you will give up if need be. Above all, plan to be flexible. A company may offer a privilege you never thought of getting that will outweigh the one you did think of asking for.

To avoid an obvious lie when asked what salary you are presently earning, say that you will need something in the $30,000 to $35,000 range, or whatever range you feel you are worth.

There is an etiquette to asking for benefits at the hiring stage. Mention those that you have received through your former employer and those that you think you will need to do the job well. Any *business* excuse for needing a benefit will do. You cannot ask a firm to pick up a country club membership tab because your spouse likes to play golf and won't be happy about relocating unless assured of a place to play. You *can* say that you need a country club membership because of the business contacts it will provide you. You *can* mention that you play tennis several times a week with an important client and would like a company membership so that you can return the client's invitations.

If the company is anxious for you to relocate fairly soon, this gives you an easy opening to mention any problems you are going to have selling your house or finding housing in a new community. A wise prospective employer will read between the lines and offer whatever he or she can. Make sure, too, that the company will pay moving expenses, although this has become a standard executive benefit. Whether or not you will need a car is usually readily agreed upon by both parties.

Sometimes you can do a little jockeying over physical position within a company during the hiring process. Usually this is only necessary in huge corporations, where office sizes and types are less than desirable even at middle-management levels. When you are shown the facilities, usually during the final interview and before you sit down to work out the final arrangements, your new employer often will indicate where you will be working. If you are not offered an office that is sufficiently large for you to work in, consider mentioning this later when the two of you sit down together. But whatever you do, don't say you need a large private office because you had one before. Give a valid business reason why you need one, something such as, "I've never worked in an open area before, and since I handle many of my sales calls by phone, I was wondering whether it would be possible to have an office that offers more privacy." Before mentioning this, though, you should realize that where you sit initially is not nearly so important as where you sit a few months later after you have had a promotion and have begun to prove yourself to the company. Then, too, companies either realize the value of privacy for employees or they don't, and arguing over office space may appear petty to a prospective employer who doesn't see the need for privacy. The executive hiring you also may be powerless, in a large company, to do anything about your office. In short, it is frequently not worth it to make a point of physical surroundings.

WAITING TO START A NEW JOB

Once you have worked out the details of your employment and set a starting date (and asked for confirmation of everything by letter), the interview will end. You have nothing official to do for the company until the day you start.

An especially gracious gesture on the part of the executive doing the hiring, however, is to maintain some contact during this period. A lunch might be arranged to introduce a new executive to colleagues, or a purely social celebration dinner might be planned. Nothing starts off a new employer-employee relationship on a better footing than making the new employee feel that the company is truly pleased to have hired him or her.

USING THE POWER TO HIRE AND FIRE GRACIOUSLY

At some point in your executive career, you will be in a position to hire and fire others. Although both these actions involve personal style, there are a few rules of etiquette that any executive should follow.

1. Keep all transactions of this nature confidential. If you decide to hire someone, that is between the two of you. If you interview someone and decide not to hire, that is still between the two of you. The same thing applies to firing. Nothing is more painful to everyone in an office than to know that someone is about to be fired. If you plan to dismiss someone for any reason, keep silent until you have told the person being dismissed. Afterward, discuss the matter as little as possible. You may need to reassure your staff or bolster morale if there are mass firings or layoffs, but there is never any reason to discuss the details of an individual case.

2. Do all the hiring and firing yourself, in person. It is a courtesy to the person involved, a kind way to end a relationship and a gracious way to begin one.

3. When dismissing someone, show respect for his or her feelings and opinions. After all, the ability to take away someone's job is the ultimate sign of power; it is more potent than giving raises, benefits, and promotions, and it can become an ego trip for you if you are not careful.

4. If possible, stretch the truth a little when firing someone for a minor offense—too many sick days, tardiness, long lunches—and let the person walk away with his or her ego intact. It is fine to tell the person what he or she has done wrong, but do not elaborate or talk at great length about the offenses.

5. Do not promise someone a recommendation that you will not be able to deliver. Mention, if asked, that the person might better seek a recommendation elsewhere. If at all possible, though, try to give someone a good recommendation, even if you have fired him or her. What you disliked may not offend another employer so badly. If you must say something unflattering, couch it tactfully and surround it with the person's good points.

When the Decision Is Not to Hire

If you decide that a certain interviewee is not what you are seeking after all, you owe it to the person to tell him or her yourself. Techniques such as suddenly becoming unavailable or leaving the talks dangling indefinitely or saying that your company won't be hiring right now after all, when you know you intend to hire someone else, are cowardly and rude.

Telephone the person or invite him or her to your office to say that you have decided not to offer the job. Avoid going into details that might hurt the person's ego unnecessarily, but give as honest an answer as you can. Instead of saying, "I don't think your personality will work in our company," you might say, "I feel that you might find yourself in conflict with the person for whom you would have to work. You are very different persons, with different management techniques, and would clash sooner or later. Your management techniques are excellent, but I would rather see you put them to work somewhere where they will be truly appreciated. Because of this, I have decided not to offer you this position. I hope you will understand."

If the person is obviously under- or overqualified, this is one of the easiest things of all to explain and hurts no one's feelings.

When You Make an Offer

If you are going to offer a position to someone, call or write the person and ask when he or she can come in to see you. At this stage of negotiations, you both will know what is going to happen. Making the job offer is the least important aspect of this interview; the real purpose of the interview is to hammer out the financial arrangements.

Sometimes an offer is formally made in a letter and reinforced with a friendly phone call, which may be followed by a brief waiting period while the prospective employee makes his or her decision about whether to accept the job. When the job has been accepted, the meeting to talk out arrangements is set up.

CHAPTER 14

Moving Up

THERE IS AN ART to resigning graciously, and in these days of executive job hopping, it is one that merits careful mastery.

But before you resign graciously, it will be necessary to pay a little attention to the etiquette of job hunting discreetly. Leaving one company to go to work for another is never a completely permanent severance. You may return to work there someday, and frequently you will find yourself using former bosses as references. Therefore it pays to leave in everyone's good graces, which is not always an easy feat, since the mere act of resignation often implies that there is something you don't like about a company or a boss.

When you find you are so unhappy with a company that it is time to get out, keep your unhappiness to yourself. This is not the time to foment a revolution, the conclusion of which is that you move on, leaving behind a wake of disgruntled colleagues. Conduct your job search quietly and use company time as little as possible. Make a polite excuse when you must take time off for an interview or an errand related to your job search.

GIVING YOUR BOSS THE NEWS

Once you have accepted an offer to go to work for another firm, make sure that you are the person who delivers the news to your boss. It is a courtesy that you owe him or her. If your boss is going to be unavailable for a few days, explain to your new boss that you would appreciate having any formal announcement held up until you have told your present employer. Then don't leak the news to anyone; it always gets out, and your boss will hear it one way or another before he or she sets foot in the office again.

If your boss is out of town for an extended period of time, you can either resign to the boss's superior or try to contact the boss by phone. Generally your boss will appreciate your making the effort to contact him or her; many a boss has shown hurt feelings when passed over in a resignation by an employee.

PLANNING TO TAKE YOUR LEAVE

When you are making arrangements with your future employer, request whatever amount of time you will need to wrap up any assignments you are working on for your present employer. This does not mean, however, that you must think in terms of finishing assignments, for once you have resigned, you will find you are a lame duck. Think, instead, of tying up loose ends and transferring your work to someone else, or of organizing your work properly so that it can be easily transferred to someone else.

Unless you are very close to being irreplaceable, two to three weeks' notice is usually sufficient. Companies don't encourage even an executive who has resigned with the best possible feelings to stay much longer than that. Then, too, the time between your resignation and your actual departure is a fairly emotional one that is best not prolonged. Pack your briefcase, tell everyone how much you have enjoyed working with them, and leave.

GIVING AND ATTENDING FAREWELL CELEBRATIONS

As a rule your colleagues or employees will plan luncheons and other festivities to say goodbye. An especially gracious gesture is to plan something for your colleagues and those who have worked for you.

By all means, you should ask anyone who has especially helped you or has been a mentor to you to lunch or dinner. While this is a time to terminate some relationships, it is also a time to strengthen friendships and even business relationships that you wish to continue. Turning the tables with some entertaining is an excellent way to do this and to say thank you.

MAINTAINING TIES

Make an effort to keep up any business or personal ties you value after you leave, for the day will surely come when you will need references for your next job, and the task of supplying references usually falls to the person who employed you several years back.

INDEX